Eccentric Culture

Eccentric Culture
A Theory of Western Civilization

Rémi Brague

Translated by Samuel Lester

ST. AUGUSTINE'S PRESS
South Bend, Indiana
2002

1 2 3 4 5 6   08 07 06 05 04 03 02

Library of Congress Cataloging in Publication Data
Brague, Rémi, 1947–
    [Europe, la voie romaine. English]
    A theory of Western civilization / Rémi Brague ;
    translated by Samuel Lester.
        p. cm.
    ISBN 1-890318-14-0 (alk.)
    1. Europe – Civilization – Roman influences. 2. Europe
    – Civilization – Greek influences. I. Title.
D1055 .B7313 2001
940 – dc21   2001001191

∞ *The paper used in this publication meets the minimum requirements of the*
International Organisation for Standardization (ISO) – Paper for
documents – Requirements for permanence – ISO 9706: 1994.

Printed in the Czech Republic by Newton Printing Ltd.   www.newtonprinting .com

Contents

I
The Constituent Divisions

When one proposes, as I do here, to speak of Europe and culture, one must first say what one means by Europe. Otherwise, one is condemned to calling everything and its contrary by this name. Thus, at the time of the Maastricht Treaty's ratification referendum in 1992, one witnessed an inflation in the number of book titles in France decorated with the noun "Europe" or the adjective "European." Often a none-too-scrupulous editor added this label to just about anything to get it to sell. And where the title actually did correspond to the content, the book touched on realities one would have been better inspired to call "industrial societies," "the Occident" (in confrontation with an "Orient," especially over economic matters), or "Modernity," or by any other name. But as for reflections on what Europe actually is – nothing.

Now, it is a reflection of just this sort that I propose to undertake here. And since I am a philosopher by trade, I belong to that race of people who are a bit obtuse, and for whom one must really "just spell out" even the clearest things – Being, the Good, the City, Man, and some other supposedly self-evident notions. I will begin, therefore, by asking myself that thick-witted question, the Socratic question – "just what is this we are talking about" – when we speak of Europe.

Content and Space

When one asks this question, one often wonders what sort of things might be considered "European." One then obtains a more or less long list of items that seem positive or negative according to each person's taste: the free market, "democracy," technology, but also imperialism, etc. It would hardly be difficult to see, then, that these phenomena are found in parts of the globe that do not belong to Europe, and even found there more often or to a higher degree than in Europe. For example, the United States had its revolution and emancipated its Jews earlier than France. Today, it is perhaps even more "democratic." Japan, for its part, is more technologically advanced than Europe. As a result, one sees two concepts of Europe appear: one, which may be called "cultural," includes a certain number of economic and political facts; the other, the geographical concept, designates a certain part of the globe that can be pointed to on a map.

What is "European," even if it is found over the whole or the greater part of the world, takes its name from its origin at one place on the globe. It would therefore seem a good method to take the "geographical" concept of Europe as a point of departure. And this is just what I will discuss in the present chapter.

Yet it is necessary to point out that the geographical approach, through which Europe appears as a space, is not really a point of departure. For the name "Europe" has designated different things throughout history even to geographers. I will distinguish here three successive meanings:

a) The first sense – the one suggested by its probably Semitic etymology – is that of a *direction*, that of the setting sun, as signified by the Arab word *Maghreb*, which may even have the same root. One cannot just show where Europe is, then, and even less define its frontiers. This sense is as old as the Phoenician maritime expansion: for the sailors of Tyre or Sidon, the other shore of the Mediterranean was located toward the west.

b) The second sense, which one finds used by Greek geographers, is that of a *space* around which one can navigate, and
in whose interior or exterior one might find oneself. More
precisely, it referred to that space extending from the western
shore of the Aegean Sea to the ocean. As long as one sticks
with one of these two senses, to be located *in the direction of*
Europe or *in* Europe is only a way of locating what one is talking about without according it any particular importance,
much less any particular value – no more than we would
accord any particular importance to the fact of living next to
odd or even addresses on our street. In this second sense,
then, we see that the adjective "European" designates no permanent quality, nor anything that we might carry away with
us, but only a simple localization that is therefore variable.
And so Herodotus, in a passage that contains the oldest
occurrence in Greek – and in all languages – of the adjective
"European" (*eurōpēios*), speaks of a tribe that, having lived
until then on the western bank of the Hellespont, established
themselves in Asia minor. He notes that they changed their
name, abandoning the one they had when they were
"Europeans."[1]

c) The third sense is that of a *whole* to which one can
belong. Being European, then, would no longer mean just
being situated in the interior of a space, but being one of the
elements constituting a whole. Only since the dream of the
reconstitution of an empire of the Occident has "Europe"
begun to designate a totality of this sort. This totality is itself
of variable extent: what was in the beginning the Western
Roman Empire[2] was enlarged until it encompassed the
Iberian peninsula and the British Isles, the Scandinavian
world, central Europe, etc., without suppressing the subtle
differences between these regions.

Distinguishing these three senses allows one to sort out

---

1   Herodotus, VII.73.

2   "l'empire romain d'Occident" [*translator's note*]

apparent contradictions. Thus, for example, Aristotle placed
Athens in Europe – that is, to the west of the Aegean Sea. But
elsewhere when he speaks of national characters, he situates
the Greeks, not *in* Europe, but rather *between* Europe and
Asia: Europe, being too cold, produces hardy but ungovern-
able peoples; Asia, being too hot, produces indolent ones at
the mercy of the first despot; temperate Greece, in contrast, is
the country of liberty.[3]

A Matter of Conscience

In this way, the idea of Europe leaves the domain of geography to enter into that of history. And this leads one to wonder
what is implied, in the next place, by this question of "what
is" with regard to Europe. This question poses a problem of
method: how does one define a reality that falls under the
province of history and geography without falling into a certain "essentialism," without making an unwarranted hypo-
stasis. For, though one may be able to construct a concept
from natural realities that don't change, how can one construct such a concept from realities that are in the domain of
history, and that are therefore, by definition, unstable and in
motion? One can attempt a philosophy of man, of virtue, of
science, etc., because these are consistent and stable realities.
But in what way would a philosophy of Europe be more prac-
ticable than a philosophy of Eure-et-Loir?[4]

I will not presuppose here anything like a Platonic idea of
Europe floating in an intelligible heaven. But at the other
extreme, I do not consider this word simply a label that might
comprehend realities totally foreign to one another. Indeed,

---

3   Respectively, Aristotle, *Physics*, V.1 (224b 21) and *Politics* VII.7 (1327b
     20–33, especially 24 ff.).

4   Eure-et-Loire is the French administrative department in the region of
     Chartres, just southwest of the department that contains Paris. [*trans-
     lator's note*]

one manages to recover, at the very least, over a somewhat extended period of time, a continuity in the use of this term. To say it in a somewhat simplified philosophical vocabulary: if one is neither Platonic nor nominalist, one can still be Aristotelian – that is, conceptualist. What one calls a concept in philosophy is translated in history as the presence of a *consciousness of belonging*. A European is one who is conscious of belonging to a whole. If one does not have this consciousness, and if one is not therefore European, this does not necessarily imply that one is a barbarian. But one is not a European without wanting to be one. To transpose what Renan said of the nation, Europe is a continual plebiscite. Even what remains in the historical consciousness, everything that is source and root, is reinterpreted from the point of view of the consciousness; and, in a certain measure, history itself is fabricated in reference to it.

This choice of consciousness as the criterion of belonging to Europe permits me to answer an objection that was made to the first edition of the present work. Prehistorians have observed the presence of common traits defining certain cultures extending throughout the European era. There would have been, then, a European unity before Charlemagne, and even before Greece, before Rome, etc. I answer: yes, of course we know that certain identical material traces (pottery, remnants of funeral rites, etc.) turn up from one end of this space to the other. But how can we know with certainty that these people were *conscious* of belonging to a whole? We share many things with the Japanese regarding technology: our computers and our cars are more or less similar. But are we nonetheless conscious of being a part of the same civilization? Before lending consciousness to a particular human group, we must have access to their linguistic traces, and this is not possible in the case of societies that antedate the written word.

Moreover, this criterion of consciousness permits one to conceive the sense of belonging to Europe in a supple and evolving way. One could ask oneself, with regard to each region, at what date and in what sense it began to consider itself European. In this way, one would be able to avoid the improper claims, the truly speculative annexations, that would enclose peoples in a space which they neither desire, nor even have an idea of . . . .

As a totality, Europe is certainly situated in a specific place on the planet. But this reference to concrete reality is nonetheless not that self-evident. Indeed, "Europe" designates a space that one has no trouble indicating with a vague sweep of the hand. But difficulties begin as soon as one tries to delimit it. The European space, in contrast to the American one, has no natural frontiers, except in the west, where they are not always perceived as such. Even if there are capes in Brittany, in Galicia, and in Cornwall called "the edge of the world," one cannot speak so simply of the inhabited space: a country such as Portugal considers itself as more open to the Atlantic than limited by it. The frontiers of Europe, as we shall see, are solely cultural.

In what follows, I shall seek to enclose the European space through a progressive approach, delimiting it with a series of dichotomies. Their network will encircle and bound off a residue that will be Europe. In this fashion, Europe will not be arrived at through union – a union that is nevertheless, for better or worse, in the process of coming about on the political and economic levels. One will attain it rather as a result of a division that separates it from what it is not. This paradox appears, in the most elementary fashion, on a geographical map. I will begin, therefore, by recalling for the record some fundamental givens, without pretending to the least originality.[5]

---

5   For this historical and geographic reminder, I exempt myself from bibliographical indications. One can find everything one needs in the historians. I limit myself to indicating only a few topical pertinent works in the notes. The importance of a chronological and geographic delimitation of Europe is underlined by O. Halecki, *The Limits and Divisions of European History* (New York: Sheed & Ward, 1950), xiv–242 pp.

Dichotomies

One can consider Europe, that is, the Europe we can point to today on a world map, as the result, the residue, of a series of dichotomies. These have taken place along two axes: one, running north to south, separates an East from a West, and an axis perpendicular to the first, running east to west, separates a North from a South. They go back several millennia. It is curious to note, though I don't attribute any particular significance to it, that these dichotomies have taken place at approximately five-century intervals.

a) The first dichotomy occurred along a north-south axis. It divided a West from an East, roughly the Mediterranean basin, on the one hand ("the Occident"), and the rest of the world (the "Orient") on the other.[6]

This dichotomy began to appear when Greece won its liberty from the Persian Empire at the time of the Persian War, and was fully operative by the time of the Hellenic conquest of the whole Mediterranean basin. This was brought about, first of all, by Alexander the Great and by the Hellenistic kingdoms that succeeded him. It was continued by the Roman conquest. From the victorious campaign of Pompey against the pirates, completed in 67 BC, until the Islamic conquest of its southern shores in the seventh and eighth centuries, the space of the Mediterranean sea was the peaceable and undivided possession of the Roman world that gave it its name. What the Romans called *mare nostrum* is still the *bahr Rûm* for Islam.

This conquest isolated an "inhabited land" (*oikoumenē*) from the rest of the universe that was considered barbarian. The frontier separating them remained in flux for a long time. The maximum eastward expansion, during the reign of Alexander, who went as far as the Indus River, was principally a military one. The Hellenization of the Orient was slow

---

6   The importance of the Mediterranean basin as the general framework of Western history no longer needs to be recalled, in particular, since the work of F. Braudel.

and mainly affected the cities. The presence of Rome in the region never could make the frontier of Hellenism coincide completely with that separating the Roman world from the Persian Empire. But even the latter, at least under the Sassanid Dynasty, experienced a Hellenistic cultural influence.

In return, the neighborhood of the "Orient" continued to exercise a certain "orientalizing" influence on the Roman world which, for example, aimed at a totalitarianism in imitation of its Parthian adversary.[7]

It was in this Mediterranean unity, starting from the beginning of our era – which besides took its definition from it – that Christianity established itself and began to call itself *catholic*, that is, universal.

b) A second division followed along an east-west axis. It took place at the interior of the Mediterranean basin, which it separated into two more or less equal halves: this was the effect of the Muslim conquest of the eastern and southern parts of the Mediterranean in the seventh century.[8]

The frontiers between these two domains have hardly moved from that period until today. At the most, the east-west axis has teetered back and forth a bit. One may ignore temporary encroachments: the incursion of the Arabic pillagers to Poitiers,[9] the occupation of Sicily by Islam, or that of Palestine by the Crusaders.

---

7   Cf. H.-I. Marrou, *Décadence romaine ou antiquité tardive?* (Paris: Seuil, 1977), p. 25.

8   Cf. the germinal essay of H. Pirenne, *"Mahomet et Charlemagne"* (1922) in *Histoire économique de l'Occident médiéval* (Paris: Desclée de Brouwer, 1951), pp. 62–70. Historians have debated, not the capital importance of the scission of the northern from the southern Mediterranean, but the consequences that the Belgian historian drew from it. Cf. the dossier of the discussion in P. E. Hübinger (ed.), *Bedeutung und Rolle des Islam beim Übergang vom Altertum zum Mittelalter* (Darmstadt: Wissenschaftliche Buchgesellschaft, 1968), xii–329 pp.

9   I would recall here of how little consequence the Battle of Poitiers was. The Muslim expansion toward the west was truly stopped, during the

Durable rectifications remained rare: one might recall the eleventh-century passage of Anatolia (to which the conquerors gave the present name, Turkey) to Islam, offset by the Christian reconquest of the Iberian peninsula completed three centuries later. The Ottoman incursions into Hungary and Austria in the sixteenth and seventeenth centuries were without lasting consequences, though they did leave more durable traces in the form of Muslim populations in Bulgaria, Bosnia, and Albania. Greece would have to wait until the nineteenth century to recover the independence it lost in the fifteenth.

Islam, for its part, did not limit itself to the Mediterranean world. It spread quite quickly, first in the seventh century toward the east, taking in Persia and central Asia; then, following the conquest of the Punjab by Mahmud of Ghazna (1020), into eastern Asia. Moving toward the south, it gradually spread into Africa. In this way, it has called into question the division of the world into an Orient and an Occident – a redistribution of space that, as we shall see further on, has had important cultural consequences. To the north and the west, Christendom was not unaffected by the proximity of the Islamic world, which opened it up, either directly to its own influences, or to those from the further reaches of the Orient.[10] And the Byzantine world, though directly in conflict with the Islamic one, developed in a constant relationship to it.[11]

Just as Islam distanced its center of gravity from the Mediterranean, realized when the Abbassid Caliphs moved their capital from Damascus to Baghdad, Christendom re-

---

same period, by the failure of the expeditions against Byzantium. Cf. B. Lewis, *The Muslim Discovery of Europe* (New York: Norton, 1982), pp. 18 ff.

10 Cf. *infra.*, chap. IV, p. 65 ff.

11 Cf. the extremely suggestive essay by G. E. von Grünebaum, "Parallelism, Convergence and Influence in the Relations of Arab and Byzantine Philosophy, Literature and Piety" in *Dumbarton Oaks Papers* 18 (1964), pp. 91–111.

centered itself further north, between the Loire and the Rhine. As to Europe, (in the current sense, the third of those that I distinguished above), the northern Mediterranean is precisely the domain where it was born. It did not limit itself to this region but spread, as is known, in two directions. On land, first with the German and then the Russian expansion, it spread into central Asia and Siberia; then on sea, by the great discoveries which brought the European colonization and peopling to the two Americas and to Oceania.

Nor did the Church limit itself to this "European" domain. Before the missions of the modern epoch to America and then Africa, Christianity was from the first also African, with the monophysitic church of Ethiopia, and Oriental, with the Nestorians of central Asia and China – not to mention the Christians of the Orient who lived under Muslim domination as a "protected" people (*ḏimmī*), or on the margins of that domination (in Armenia and Georgia).

c) One witnesses then a third division[12] that took place in the interior of Christendom along the north-south axis. This was the schism between the Latin and Byzantine, a schism that arose on the religious level perhaps as soon as the 10th Century, in any case in 1054, and reached a point of no return in 1204 when the soldiers of the Fourth Crusade took Constantinople. It established a tension between a Catholic West and an Orthodox East that would continue to increase.

This division took place in the interior of a world that remained Roman and Christian, and ran along a preexisting line of cleavage dating from the pagan epoch. Its beginning coincided largely with the division that separated the Western Empire – in which Latin was the language of administration, commerce, and culture – from the Eastern Empire which, though it was administered until quite late in Latin, used

---

12   O. Halecki, himself a Pole, showed how much prudence must be taken in practicing this division. Cf. *op. cit.* chap. VI: "The Geographical Divisions (a) Western and Eastern Europe," pp. 105–22. Cf. J. Szúcs, "The Three Historical Regions of Europe. An Outline," *Acta Historica Academiae Scientiarum Hungaricae* 29 (1983), pp. 131–84.

Greek as the principal language of culture. The division then extended toward the north at the moment of the conversion of the Slavs.[13] They varied in their choices, some swinging toward the Latin side of Christianity (the Poles, Czechs, Croats, Slovenes, Slovaks, etc.), as the Hungarians, Scandinavians, and finally the Lithuanians had also done, while others swung to the Greek side (Russians, Serbs, Bulgarians), as did the Romanians. This division would not really be challenged, in the cultural sphere, even by the emergence in the seventeenth and eighteenth centuries of churches attached to the Roman seat (and called "uniate" by their adversaries), as for example, in the Ukraine.

This division took place as well in the interior of a Christendom that had come to lodge itself in the Roman world and which was tied to it. It divided the Church that until then had maintained its orthodoxy in confrontation with the Nestorian and Jacobite heresies, as well as its fidelity to the Empire (whence the name "Melchite" that the Church received among the Arameans). The schism split in two what had until then remained undivided. But with a single blow it formed Europe. After the Oriental schism, the word "catholic" began to take on a different meaning. And so the Church that called itself by this adjective came to cover more or less what we call Europe today: two halves, central and western, of a whole which extends to the east of Poland, and that were only divided after the war, as is evident today, in a totally artificial manner.

As to the Orthodox world, and especially Russia, it is not at all self-evident that it belongs to Europe – to either one or the other side.[14] The slogan "Europe from the Atlantic to the

---

13 In this field, one book helped me to understand how little I knew: A. and J. Sellier, *Atlas des peuples d'Europe centrale* (Paris: La Découverte, 1991), 192 pp.

14 On the reticence of Westerners during the Renaissance to integrate Russia within Europe, see D. Hay, *Europe. The Emergence of an Idea* (Edinburgh University Press, 1957), p. 123.

Urals" is that of a western European, De Gaulle. In the east, this membership is entirely a matter of an internal debate, secular, but still ongoing, between Slavophile and Occidentalist tendencies.

d) Finally, the last division took place along an east-west axis following the Reformation. I prefer this term, which allows one to distinguish the events that followed 1517 from the many reforms in the history of the Church, including the Catholic reform tied to the Council of Trent which came about in response to the Reformation. In the sixteenth century, the Reformation led to the separation of the Protestant from the Catholic domain. Roughly speaking, the north passed to Lutheran or Calvinist Protestantism (Scandinavia and Scotland), while England chose through Anglicanism not to choose at all. The south (Spain, Portugal, and Italy) remained Catholic. The center remained in dispute. In Germany, as others have remarked, the Reformation resonated especially in areas situated beyond the frontier of the Roman Empire (*limes*). France remained undecided for a long time. Along the Danube, too, frontiers took some time to establish themselves: a good part of it passed to Protestantism but was reconquered by Catholicism in the seventeenth century, though not without leaving lingering resentment, as in Bohemia.

This division took place in the interior of Occidental Christendom, and as this coincided with Europe, it didn't put Europe's existence into question. But Europe found itself divided along with Christendom. In this way, the Reformed world is just as decidedly European as the Catholic world, a fact that I underline here in order to avoid misunderstandings about the adjective "Roman," which I will shortly define with greater precision.

A Scarred Memory

Europe thus presents us with a scarred face that preserves the traces of the wounds that formed it. The Europeans must preserve the memory of their scars, for they play a double role. First, the scars define them in relation to what is not Europe; secondly, they split Europe from within. Preserving the memory of these divisions can keep us from falling into several errors.

Generally, one should avoid juxtaposing too quickly the dichotomies that have been practiced, especially when formed along axes oriented in the same way. The most serious source of confusion is without doubt that which comes from the use of the word "Orient" as opposed to "Occident." *Ex Oriente caligo.* Indeed, even if the words corresponded, the ancient distinction between Orient and Occident doesn't coincide at all with the Roman Orient and Occident, nor yet with the Christian one. It coincides even less with the one that opposes an occidental Europe to the "Orient" of Orientalism – in which Morocco is oriental, but Greece, occidental – an opposition one might denominate by the old terms of *"Ponant"*[15] and "Levant." The distinctions I am making here, it seems to me, help one avoid the myths surrounding the "Orient" in general – for the counter images against which Europe has often been tempted to define itself flow through these myths.[16]

Before entering into the details, however, we should recall a few important points:

a) The first division (the opposition between the Mediterranean basin and the rest of the world) does not have the same status as those that follow. The later divisions, in

---

15   In French, the direction of the setting sun, i.e., the West, as Levant originally indicated the direction of the rising sun. [*translator's note*].

16   The literature on this subject is vast – excessive, no doubt. Cf. for example the fashionable work of E. Said, *Orientalism* (New York: Pantheon Books, 1978), xi–368 pp. with the considerably more serious response of B. Lewis, "The Question of Orientalism," in *Islam and the West* (Oxford: Oxford University Press, 1993), pp. 99–118, and T. Hentsch, *L'Orient imaginaire. La vision politique occidentale de l'Est méditerranéen* (Paris: Minuit, 1988), 290 pp.

fact, place entities of the same status, which consider themselves as unities, on opposite sides of the same border. Thus,
though Islamic civilization is rich in its diversity of peoples
and languages, it conceives of itself, in its political-theological
theory, as a united world, "pacified" (*dār as-salām*) in a common "war" against paganism (*dār al-ḥarb*) and, according to
certain authors, in a common "truce" with the other
monotheisms (*dār aṣ-ṣulḥ*). Similarly, the Orthodox,
Protestant, and Catholic worlds feel that they themselves
form unities in relation to the others. Each unity thus defines
itself in relation to another unity. But what about the
"Orient"? Does the Orient like to think of itself as a unity? Is
it conscious of forming one? Into what grab-bag could one
collect the Indian world with those that spread from it, Tibet,
Indonesia or Southeast Asia, and the Chinese world with its
spheres of cultural influence, Japan, Korea, etc.? Conceived as
a unity, the "Orient" is hardly more than a mirage or a foil, at
least as used by Occidentals. Besides, it was just along these
lines that the most intelligent of the Greeks perceived the situation: Plato made fun of the division of humanity into
Greeks and barbarians – a division parallel to that dividing
the animal kingdom between man and the rest of the living
creatures.[17]

Thus, I applaud the effort to reintegrate the memory of
the very different cultures we assemble into one "Oriental"
bag, and in particular, the effort to make a first step toward
this recollection – by becoming conscious that we have forgotten.[18] But I myself will not run the risk here of speaking of
what distinguishes the Occident from the Orient. First of all,
for the reason I've mentioned, the "Orient" does not seem to
me to constitute a true entity. And secondly, because I do not
have any first-hand access to these cultural traditions.

---

17 Cf. Plato, *Statesman* 262d.

18 Cf. R.-P. Droit, *L'oubli de l'Inde. Une amnésie philosophique* (Paris: Presses
Universitaires de France, 1989), 262 pp.

I will satisfy myself with a single remark that is not outside of my aim here: preserving the memory of this distinction precludes confounding the Occident with Christendom. Christianity has in fact a universal vocation, and it does not limit itself to the geographical area that it covers at any given moment: the "Christians of Saint Thomas" in Malabar and the Ethiopians can hardly be considered "Occidentals."

b) The second division (the opposition between the Christian north and the Muslim south) precludes confusing Christendom with Greco-Latin culture. Islamic civilization itself also inherited from this culture to a large extent: its birthplace on the Arabian peninsula was already hellenized in part,[19] and after the conquest of Iraq and Syria, it installed itself in a cultural domain prepared first by the Hellenistic kingdoms, and then by Byzantium, from which it also adopted some elements (for example, in its administration – the mail service, the currency, etc.).[20] Some have even ventured the formula: "No Alexander the Great, no Islamic civilization!"[21] It may even be that some dimensions of the Muslim world are, one might say, more "ancient" than our occidental world. One example: the Turkish bath. The phrase suffices to set off in the mind of an Occidental a train of auditory and olfactory stereotypes tied to what passes for "typically Arabic." But what is a Turkish bath if not the ancient thermae forgotten in the Occident, but preserved in the Orient?

---

19   Cf. G. W. Bowersock, *Hellenism in Late Antiquity*, T. S. Jerome Lectures (Ann Arbor, Michigan, 1990), chap. VI.

20   On the other hand, it seems that Roman law left only a few traces on Muslim law, contrary to what one has believed since Goldziher. Cf. P. Crone, *Roman, Provincial and Islamic Law: The Origins of the Islamic Patronate* (Cambridge University Press, 1987), 178 pp.

21   C. H. Becker, "Der Islam als Problem" (1910), in *Vom Werden und Wesen der islamischen Welt. Islamstudien* (Leipzig: Quelle & Meyer, 1924), vol. 1, p. 16. Cf. also the whole essay "Der Islam im Rahmen einer allgemeinen Kulturgeschichte," *ibid.*, pp. 24–39, which forcefully defends the Islamic world's membership in the Occident.

c) The third division (the opposition of the Greek Orthodox East to a Latin Catholic West) precludes confounding Christianity with a culture, even one of determinate customs. Actually, the difference on the level of customs leaves intact some common elements that one may consider decisive. A communion on the essential level actually continues between the two churches (if one considers that they really form two separate ones): each Church recognizes the legitimacy of the sacraments of the other.[22] And this mutual recognition brings along with it a recognition of the validity of the succession of bishops starting from the apostles, and of the legitimacy of the ministries that are tied to it (*communio in sacris*).

d) The fourth division (between the Protestant North and the Catholic South) invites us not to confuse two things: the affirmation according to which the Catholic Church has received promises not to make mistakes about the essence of the message, with the rejection of the presence – other than within it – of authentic elements of this message that it must develop better.

A Graduated Membership

If I propose to recall to memory here the divisions that constitute the European unity, it is in order to raise afresh the question of European identity – and to subvert it.

A culture defines itself in relation to the people and to the phenomena it considers as its "others." One can proceed in the same way for Europe. But in this case, we find ourselves facing several "others" that one cannot reduce to an undifferentiated fall-guy or foil. Europe's "otherness" in relation to each of its different "others" does not appear to be on the same level.

---

22 The recognition by the Orthodox Churches of the Catholic sacraments is not always evident on the level of principle. In any event, the practice is not.

Europe, to the extent that it is Occidental, is the "other" of the Orient. But it shares this otherness with the Muslim world in having the Greco-Latin heritage in common.

As Christendom, Europe is the "other" of the Muslim world. Yet it shares this otherness with the Orthodox world with which it has Christianity in common.

To the extent that it is Latin Christendom, Europe is the "other" of the Byzantine world, a Greek culture. Now Europe shares this last otherness with no one: the separation of the Catholic and Protestant worlds took place within the confines of Latin Christendom – even if the Protestant world defines itself in opposition to a Church called "Roman."

I would therefore like to introduce a gradation into the idea of Europe: Europe is a variable notion. One is more or less European. Thus, if the Protestant world seems to me just as European as the Catholic, the membership of the Oriental world, traditionally Greek and Orthodox, seems to me to pose a problem.

The East of Europe

Here the problem is how to determine to what extent the regions that make up this world conform themselves to the Byzantine cultural model. Their fidelity to the oriental version of Christianity does not automatically mean that they remain within the wake of Byzantine civilization.

And it is here that one must make a distinction: Byzantium never considered itself "European." It always thought of itself as "Roman," and even as continuing the Empire with a second Rome. This claim was, by the way, entirely legitimate, as Constantine decided to transfer the capital of the Empire there in 330. Furthermore, Byzantium always considered itself as belonging to Christendom. The transfer of the seat of the Empire was also to symbolize a distancing from paganism. Here also, one finds no reason to deny that it belongs. On the other hand, in the course of its

history, Byzantium never understood the entity "Europe" to
be something it belonged to. For the Byzantines too, the word
designated Latin Christendom. Let's consider some examples: Georgios (Gennadios) Scholarios, when he refers to
Latin authors, calls them *eurōpaioi*. It is thus that he opposes
the "Europeans" – among whom, we might note, he places
the Tunisian Saint Augustine – and the "Asiatics," including
the Egyptian Saint Cyril of Alexandria.[23] Michael Apostolis, a
Greek of the fifteenth century, still compared Greece and
Europe – to the advantage of the former.[24]

    That said, what about the Orthodox nations that, after the
fall of Constantinople (1453), have known more than five centuries of turbulent history? It is clear that one cannot purely
and simply identify them with Byzantium, and this is the case
despite the fact that the Byzantine paternity is sometimes
maintained with sharp insistence. One must, then, begin by
evaluating the relative importance of the Byzantine influence
in traditionally Orthodox countries. Take Russia for example.
We can abstract from the legend according to which Moscow
is a third Rome, inheriting from both the Rome of Latium and
the one on the Bosphorus. This story was spread at the end of
the fifteenth century to legitimize the power of the Tsars. But
even without it, the path that supposedly led from Byzantium
to modern times is quite sinuous. On more than one point, the
Byzantine filiation of Russia is specious, or at least mounted
on the head of a pin, while other influences, whether from
Scandinavia or from the Mongols, have for a long time been
excluded from the official history – both Tsarist and Leninist.
I will satisfy myself with a single example: when Ivan III took
Novgorod (1478) and began to proclaim that Moscow must be

---

23 *Treatise on the Soul*, I, §6, ed. Petit *et al.*, vol. 1, p. 468, or the preface to
     his translation of *De ente et essentia, ibid.*, VI, 177 ff. (I owe this, and the
     following note, to Marie-Hélène Congourdeau.)

24 Cf. B. Laourdas, "Michel Apostolis, 'Discours sur la Grèce et l'Europe'
     (Greek)," in *Epetèris Etaireias Byzantinôn Spoudôn* 19 (1949) pp. 235–44,
     edition pp. 239–44. Cf. especially §4, p. 243.

the third Rome, and therefore the direct heir of Constantinople, he named a new bishop, Gennadius. Gennadius realized that his Bible was not complete, and had the missing books translated into Old Church Slavonic – translated, however, not from the Greek Septuagint, but from the Latin Vulgate.[25]

Does it go without saying, then, that these nations belong to Europe? Moreover, does it go without saying that they themselves think so? When did their desire to belong first appear – and was this only to claim the name? One would have to introduce infinite qualifications to try to decide the question – and repeatedly according to the region and the period, which I am not competent to do. In any event, the "Europeanness" of these regions does not go without saying: at the beginning of the century, the Jews of Bulgaria still dreamed of Austria-Hungary as "Europe."[26] And even today, an Athenian who embarks for Paris or Rome says that he is going *stin Evropi*. For me this is not a question of excluding the traditionally Orthodox countries from Europe by a decided act of denial. But neither should it be a question of annexing them, despite themselves, to a unity that they do not feel themselves members of. Not belonging to Europe does not in any event throw them into the outer darkness of some sort of barbarism. I do not at all identify Europe with the civilized world. To be outside of it is not to be inferior to it.

Finally, the observation of the possible exteriority of these countries in relation to Europe should arise solely from cultural history and should not, in consequence – it goes without saying – have anything to do with contemporary problems of an economic, political, or strategic nature, etc., on which I claim no competence to say anything whatever: whether it is

---

25 I owe this detail to the friendship of Mr. Yves Hamant (University of Paris X-Nanterre).

26 Cf. the memoirs of Elias Canetti, *Die gerettete Zunge. Geschichte einer Jugend* (Fischer Taschenbuch Verlag, 1984), p. 114, and *Die Fackel im Ohr. Lebensgeschichte 1921–1931, ibid.*, 1991, p. 81.

necessary or not to extend the frontiers of the so-called "European" Community to the countries of the ex-East – and even to Turkey; or whether it is necessary or not to help out the peoples of the former USSR – whose misfortune, let us recall, did not arise out of the "Slavic soul," but from an ideology of European origin.

A European Identity?

The preceding considerations, which might seem to come under the province of history and geography alone, have a larger compass. Actually, they bring to a meditation on Europe nothing less than the object itself. I began by reexamining a banal distinction between two concepts of Europe: Europe as place, and Europe as content. One can now see how they are articulated on top of one another. As place, Europe is the space that I have tried to close in on through a series of dichotomies that are clearly the province of geography – an intellectual and spiritual one. As content, Europe is the whole set of historically identifiable facts that have occurred in the interior of this place. These events may have been of limited duration or may have extended over long periods. They have all contributed more or less to the physiognomy of what we qualify as "European." We sometimes use this adjective to designate populations or cultural developments that were situated or still are situated outside of the frontiers of Europe. But we do so only to relate it back to realities that find their origin in the European space. Europe as "place" therefore precedes Europe as "content."

An example will help me to clarify this distinction. One speaks of "European sciences" (Husserl) or of "European technology," or yet again of "Occidental Metaphysics" (Heidegger) – and here again one means "European." The cultural realities that one designates in this way do not limit themselves to the European space, neither in their origin nor in their ultimate expansion. Science in general has appeared elsewhere than in Europe – for example, in China. And what Europe itself assimilated in mathematics and philosophy was first of all Greek, and secondly Arabic. Mathematical physics, on the other hand, appeared first in Europe with the revolution attached to the name of Galileo. And similarly, technology and industrial mechanization followed in its wake. Similarly, democracy first appeared in Greece. But it was only in the interior of the European space that it progressively eliminated the restrictions that had limited it to a small citizen elite, excluding slaves and women. One can say the same thing of the Enlightenment, in any event, in its modern form. Nothing here forbids recognizing the evidence that these phenomena are typically European, and that under their guise Europe manifested itself, and continues to manifest itself, whether as liberating or burdensome, to the rest of the world.

These phenomena were in any case born in the interior of a space that already existed and which they therefore did not create. Moreover, one can wonder whether their emergence is not tied to what defined Europe in separating it from these "others" by a more than accidental relationship. And so, we must first know what Europe is, and in this case, where Europe is, before assessing its history.

We can restate, then, the classic question of identity. One commonly wonders: who are we? And one might answer: Greeks, or Romans, or Jews, or Christians. Or, in a sense, a little of each. One has therefore been able to give all these answers, and none are false. I propose here only to introduce a little order. What principle of classification should one follow? The most suitable, on first view, is without doubt to ask the question, what do we possess that is our "own"? Certainly not humanity as it is defined in general: the so-called "barbarian" Orient and the Hellenized Occident both have that in common. Nor can we find this uniqueness in Hellenism: both the Muslim world and Byzantium are also its heirs. Nor in Judaism, which was present also outside the borders of the Mediterranean from very early on. Nor in Christianity, which the Christian Orient confesses as well.

It is however a fact, so historically important that I recall it here only for the record: Christendom did not conceive of itself, and has not been perceived by other civilizations, as Greek or as Jewish, but rather as *Roman*. The Greeks themselves, from the Byzantine period on, considered themselves Romans, and even now refer to the language they speak as "Romaic." The Muslim world called the Byzantines, who were Greek or Syriac in language, "Rumis," and the Ottoman Empire called what we ourselves call "European" Turkey the "Rumelia."

As to Europe in the narrow sense, it has a trait that is perhaps unique to it, which Europe alone claims, and that no one disputes its claim to: her Romanity – or more precisely, her *Latinity*. For "Romanity" has been claimed by Byzantium in so far as it continued the Eastern Roman Empire, and as a "second Rome," and then later by Moscow which pretended also to claim the title of the "third Rome." It was even claimed by the Ottoman Empire when the Sultan of Istanbul laid claim to the succession of the defeated emperors of Constantinople under the title of "Sultan of Rome." But no one other than Europe has wanted Latinity.

Plan

The essay that follows defends the thesis that Europe is essentially Roman by showing that the otherness through which it defined itself can be summed up starting from its "Latinity." I will try to bring to light how Europe distinguishes itself from what it is not through the "Latin" or "Roman" character of the sources it draws on.

I will show, first of all, how one can characterize something as the Roman attitude in general (chapter II).

Chapter III will show how the relation of Europe – as Christendom – to the Old Testament is a "Roman" relation, and how it distinguishes itself on this level from the Muslim world.

Chapter IV will show how the relation of Europe – as a Latin world – to its Greek sources is also "Roman," and how it distinguishes itself as such, not only from Islam, but from the Byzantine world as well.

Chapter V will show how Europe maintains a singular relationship to its own identity: its own is what it has appropriated from what was once foreign to it.

Chapter VI will consider the nature and the causes of the European paradox: what does it mean to have one's source outside of oneself? How does this come about?

In chapter VII, I will propose a few rules for a salubrious relationship between Europe and its proper identity.

Chapter VIII will try to understand in what sense the Catholic Church merits the qualification "Roman," and how it distinguishes itself on this level, not only from Islam, not only from Byzantium, but also from the Reformed world as well.

Finally, to conclude, I will ask to what extent and under what conditions the "Roman" model can remain actual, and what temptations it will have to confront.

II
Romanity as Model

One is accustomed to look for what is proper to Europe.[1] What is proper to it must single it out in relation to everything that it is not, and at the same time, reassemble everything that makes it up by distinguishing it from what is foreign to it and doesn't enter into its original formula. What is proper to Europe must therefore constitute its unity; it is the common acceptance of its "own" that must permit the European unity to establish itself. Now, this relation of Europe to what is proper to it contains a paradox.

A Proper Double

Indeed, when one wonders what is proper to Europe, and what one might expect would assure it a sense of cultural unity, one notices – and not without irony – that the question about unity receives a double response. Europe's unity arises

---

1   Generally, the word "propre" in French has a similar gamut of meanings as in English, but the most prominent sense in French, besides "neat or clean," is what is one's own, or what is most characteristic of a thing, while in English the first sense we think of is what is something's appropriateness or suitability, its correctness. Generally, where the senses overlap sufficiently, I will translate the word as "proper," although at times I must use the word "own" or a similar variant. See especially Rémi Brague's comment on the related meanings at the beginning and throughout ch. 7 below. [*Translator's note*]

not from the presence of a single element, but from two. Its culture comes down to two elements that cannot be reduced to one another. These two elements are the Jewish and later Christian tradition, on the one hand, and the tradition of pagan antiquity on the other. "Athens and Jerusalem" has been proposed as an expression to symbolize each of these currents with a proper name.[2] This opposition is founded on the opposition of Jew and Greek, borrowed from Saint Paul.[3] It was next formulated by Tertullian in the context of a polemic against Greek philosophy.[4] It was then laicized and systematized, in a somewhat recent period, under various names: "Hellene and Nazarene" in Heine,[5] "Atticism and Judaism" in S. D. Luzzatto,[6] and then "Hebraism and Hellenism" in Matthew Arnold.[7] Finally, it attained the dimensions of a conflict between two visions of the world in Lev Shestov who chose it as a title.[8]

Attempts have been made to isolate the content proper to each of these two elements. The ways of accomplishing this vary: one can oppose Athens to Jerusalem as the religion of beauty to that of obedience, as aesthetics to ethics, or yet again as reason to faith, autonomous investigation to tradi-

---

2   On this theme, cf. my article "Athens, Jerusalem, Mecca. Leo Strauss's "Muslim" Understanding of Greek Philosophy," *Poetics Today* 19 (1998), pp. 237–59.

3   Romans 1:16, 3:9, 10:12; 1 Corinthians 1:24, 10:32, 12:13; Galatians 3:28; Colossians 3:11.

4   Tertullian, *De praescriptionibus ad haereticos*, ch. VII; *Patrologiae Cursus, series Latina* 3, 23a.

5   H. Heine, *Ludwig Börne. Eine Denkschrift* (1837–39), I, then II, 8 – fourth "Letter from Helgoland" (July 29, 1830) – in *Ein deutsches Zerwürfnis*, ed. H. M. Enzensberger (Nordlingen: F. Greno, 1986), p. 128, 157 ff.

6   S. D. Luzzatto, "Atticisme et judaïsme" (first draft of January 18, 1838), published in *Otsar Nechmad* IV (1863), p. 131 ff.

7   M. Arnold, *Culture and Anarchy* (1869), ch. IV.

8   L. Chestov, *Athens and Jerusalem*. tr. B. Martin (Athens: Ohio University Press, 1966), 447 pp. (The original Russian version was written in 1937 and published in 1952).

tion, etc.[9] In any event, a polarity has been made of the difference, and the essence of each of the two elements has been sought in what most radically opposes the one to the other. As a result, the tension has become a painful fracture in the unity of European culture. Nothing, then, is more tempting than to attempt to reserve a place for one of the two elements as a legitimate ancestor while rejecting the other as being merely adventitious. However, these are the *two* elements that make Europe live by the very dynamism their tension maintains. This idea of a fecund and even constituent conflict has been most recently and remarkably defended by Leo Strauss.[10]

The Third Term: The Roman

In all these attempts, one has most often neglected a third term. Now this third term is just what seems to me to furnish the best paradigm for thinking about the relationship between Europe and what is proper to it. It is a matter of the last of the three languages (and languages, as one knows, are more than linguistic) which received an exemplary value from having most accurately expressed, on the placard Pilate had fixed to the Cross, He who hung there: the Latin, or rather, as the Evangelist has it, the "Roman" (John 19:20). Therefore, I propose the following thesis: *Europe is not only Greek, nor only Hebrew, nor even Greco-Hebraic. It is just as decidedly Roman.* "Athens and Jerusalem" – admittedly – but also Rome.[11] By this, I do not mean to throw out here, yet once

---

9   Goethe, "Israel in der Wüste," beginning, in *Noten und Abhandlungen zu besserem Verständnis des Westöstlichen Diwans.*

10   L. Strauss, "Jerusalem and Athens. Some Preliminary Reflections" (1967), in *Studies in Platonic Political Philosophy* (Chicago: University of Chicago Press, 1983), pp. 147–73. Cf. J. R. Sales i Coderch and J. Montserrat i Molas, *Introducció a la lectura de Leo Strauss* (Barcelonesa d'edicions, 1991), pp. 7–62.

11   M. Serres, *Rome. Le Livre des fondations* (Paris: Grasset, 1983), pp. 65–69. In a not entirely limpid meditation, the author defends Rome against the exclusive fascination for Athens and Jerusalem.

again, the banal evidence of the presence of a Roman influence among the other sources of our culture. This idea, now become hackneyed, has been expressed most magnificently in a few phrases of Valéry. Citing them exempts me from having to repeat more lifeless versions. Therefore, as we read in the famous note of 1924 to "The Crisis of the Spirit":

> Everywhere the names Caesar, Gaius, Trajan, and Virgil – everywhere the names Moses and Saint Paul – everywhere the names Aristotle, Plato, and Euclid have had simultaneously both meaning and authority – there is Europe. Every race and every land that has been successively Romanized, Christianized, and submitted, in matters of spirit, to the discipline of the Greeks, is absolutely European.[12]

Three ingredients, then, are necessary to make Europe: Rome, Greece, and Christianity – to which Valéry does not forget to add its sub-basement in the Old Testament. I do not want to privilege here the Roman element, nor do I want to suggest that it be constituted as the synthesis of the two others. I claim, more radically, that *we are not and cannot be "Greeks" and "Jews" unless we are first of all Romans.*

In proposing to reflect here on what the Roman character of Europe might be, I am conscious of involving myself in a domain charged with affects, both positive and negative. Before proposing a determinate concept of what is Roman and of just how Europe is Roman, it is important to make oneself aware of these affects which otherwise risk to cloud this new concept and to reduce it once again to what are sadly habitual misrepresentations. These affects are both positively and negatively charged, and their interference produces a troubling ambivalence.

---

12 P. Valéry, "La crise de l'esprit," *Œuvres* (Bibliothèque de la Pléiade, vol. 1, pp. 988–1014, and especially p. 1007 ff. and 1013 (cited).

Who's Afraid of the Big Bad She-Wolf?

On the negative side, the image of the Romans is repugnant to the entire modern sensibility. One can identify an enormous disgust with imprecise edges on the part of some whose opposition appears as only a special case – sometimes manifest as a religious opposition to a Catholic Church that one then calls *Roman* Catholicism, sometimes as a political opposition – Anglican or Gallican – to Papal centralism. The Romans of history pass for thick-haired and thick-headed rural people, not to say a rustic one, for a people of soldiers, not to say of roughnecks. If one goes so far as to concede that they had a certain political genius, one reproaches them for the centralizing imperialism that was its fruit.

Whence one sees a series of attempts to exorcise this embarrassing ancestor. In France, in particular, one witnessed the comic spectacle of a depreciation of the Romans in favor of the Gauls, and one made by people who speak a language descended directly from Latin. We are familiar with the different registers this tune has been played out in, from the sixteenth century to Ernest Lavisse and the Albums of Astérix. We are also familiar with the cultural context in which this representation was formed: it was necessary to give a set of common ancestors and a common ideology to the "French nation" that had just been invented. As to the partisans of the Greek origin of the Celts, in the sixteenth century it was a matter of thwarting the pretensions of the Hapsburg dynasty who called themselves "Roman."[13] On the other hand, the anti-Christian founders of the Third Republic, wanting to avoid a history that began with the conversion of Clovis and the Frankish tribe that would ultimately give its name to France, chose instead the Gauls, some centuries earlier, as ancestors. One thus uncoupled the birth of the nation from its baptism. Besides, choosing Vercingetorix, the hero of the sup-

---

13   Cf. B. Cerquiglini, *La Naissance du français* (Paris: Presses Universitaires de France, 1991), p. 11 ff.

posedly national struggle against the Romans, permitted a dig at the bed of Catholicism, against which the Republic wanted to affirm itself.[14]

This negative attitude was counterbalanced by a vision that esteemed the Romans in the name of the values they were supposed to represent. The rhetoric of the French Revolution is filled with Roman culture, and the arts of that epoch go so far as to ape the architecture and the furniture of the Romans. One thus wants to take inspiration from the civic virtue of a Brutus or from the patriotism of a Regulus. First the Consulate, then the Empire (how revealing are both names!) carried out a massive injection of Roman symbols into the army ("legion," "eagle," etc.) and of Roman law into the Napoleonic Code. All tended to exalt order, the patriarchal family, and the fatherland. A century later, Italian fascism undertook, with a great deal of jawboning, the exaltation of Roman virility and conquest. It may be that the image of the Romans has suffered more yet from what was promoted in such efforts. André Suarès was right to give this myth the name of a peculiar illness: the Romanitis.[15]

Nothing Invented?

Even if we get beyond the aforementioned affects, we find the same devaluation on the more dispassionate level of speculation: those who present the Greek and the Jewish as parallels, whether to oppose them or to exalt them together, have a marked tendency to neglect the Roman. The Romans invented nothing. This is exactly what a text of the great historian of Judaism says so magnificently:

14 Cf. C. Amalvi, *De l'art et la manière d'accommoder les héros de l'histoire de France. Essais de mythologie nationale* (Paris: Albin Michel, 1988), pp. 53–87.

15 In French, "la romanite." [*translator's note*] A. Suarès, *Vues sur l'Europe* (Paris: Grasset, 1991), originally published 1939, no. XXIII, p. 56.

What, then, is the origin of the high elevation of moral views that the civilized people of today's world boast? They themselves didn't produce it; they are the happy heirs who have speculated with their inheritance from Antiquity and made it grow. There are two creator peoples who were the authors of this noble morality, who have raised mankind up and brought him out of his primitive state of barbarism and savagery: the Hellenes and the Israelites. There is no third. The Latin people created nothing and transmitted nothing other than the strict order of a civilized society and a developed art of war. Besides, it was only at a decrepit age that they performed the service of some helpful insects by transporting some preexisting pollen to a fertile soil already prepared to receive it. But only the Greeks and the Hebrews have been creators, founders of a superior civilization, and only them.[16]

One may smile at the rhetoric. One may have a nostalgic sigh before the noble ingenuity with which Graetz throws a complacent eye on the accomplishments of occidental civilization. One may disagree with the vision of the whole of human history as a struggle between the Enlightenment and the Kingdom of Darkness. Nonetheless, the fact remains that the Roman contribution has been modest. It is not surprising, then, that the "roman" has so rarely been hypostatized and accorded the honors of a capital letter to become "the Roman." Philosophers have reflected only a little on the Roman experience. And where they have done so, it has been in a very negative way. Such was the case with Heidegger.[17] This was also true for Simone Weil who, in a manner quite

---

16   H. Graetz, *Geschichte der Juden . . .* , introduction, vol. 1 (Leipzig: 1874), p. xx.

17   Cf. especially the course on Parmenides from the Winter Semester 1942–1943 (Gesamtausgabe 54). A first orientation may be found in E. Escoubas, "La question romaine, la question impériale. Autour du tournant," in *Heidegger. Questions ouvertes* (Paris: Osiris, 1988), pp. 173–88.

interesting besides for our concern here, drew a parallel between Rome and Israel in order to express her reprobation of both together as supposedly incarnating the same "great beast." One can cite little more than the case of Hannah Arendt as a very brilliant exception to this tendency.[18] In practice, it has not been rare that the movement of rediscovery of classical antiquity since Winckelmann has reaffirmed its desire to skip over the Roman to go directly back to the Greek source. And it is understandable . . . if the Romans are really as uninteresting as it is claimed.

One could rush to the defense of the Romans by enumerating the long list of their contributions to European culture. This would be fastidious and hardly original. But moreover, one would only manage in this way to grasp the *content* of Roman culture, that one would lend a specificity to, without managing to grasp the *form*. In one cultural domain, everyone concedes that the Romans have invented and passed on a significant contribution to posterity: the *law*.[19] This fact is recognized; it is of great importance, though I can do little more than note it here. But once the evidence is acknowledged, the paradox repeats itself: law is rightly what regulates transactions. By permitting the circulation of wealth, it frees up the time that would be required for each to produce everything individually, and permits the allocation of that time to the creation of new goods. We will see further on how this unique "content" of Romanity finds an analogue in a determinate model of a relationship to culture as the transmission of what is received.

Howsoever this may be, the few juridical concepts whose Roman paternity we do not question will soon appear quite

18 See the comments in B. Cassin, "Grecs et Romains: les paradigmes de l'Antiquité chez Hannah Arendt," in *Ontologie et Politique. Hannah Arendt* (Tierce, 1989), pp. 17–39, especially pp. 22–26.

19 The French word *droit* has a wider meaning than the English *law*, particularly encompassing *right* as well. [*Translator's note*.] Just one citation from an infinite bibliography: Ph. Cormier, *Généalogie de personne* (Paris: Critérion, 1994), ch. III, particularly p. 107.

meager and even primitive compared to the richness of the Greek contribution, on the one hand, and to the developed form these elements have acquired in the course of European history, on the other. And so, when one tries to grasp the content of the Roman experience, one arrives at little more than a bastardized transposition of the Greek, or at a rudimentary sketch of what is medieval or modern. The Roman, from this point of view, can only appear to have succeeded at this paradox of being both decadent and primitive at the same time.

All that the most severe judges concede to Romanity is to have spread the riches of Hellenism and to have transmitted it down to us. But this is precisely the important fact – everything changes if one stops examining the content of the Roman experience only, and instead turns to the transmission itself. This one little thing that is conceded to be properly Roman is perhaps the whole of Rome. This is precisely the content of the Roman contribution: the structure of the transmission of a content not properly its own. The Romans have done little more than transmit, but that is far from nothing. They have brought nothing new in relation to those two creator peoples, the Greeks and the Hebrews. But they were the bearers of that innovation. They brought innovation itself. What was ancient for them, they brought as something new.

The People of Departure

Now I maintain that such a manner of bringing is not purely accidental and contingent, a result of historical chance only. It is, for me, the center of the Roman experience. The diffusion of Greek and Hebrew heritage therefore found a particularly fertile ground in Rome. One can try to describe this experience. I will do so without pretending to objectivity, but on the contrary, by isolating particular features in function of my aim.

The Roman experience is, first of all, one of space. There the world was seen from the point of view of a subject who looks forward, forgetting what is behind him. This way of seeing is reflected in the mapping of the reality presupposed by language. Thus, the same word (*altus*) signifies equally well both "high" and "profound"; what the language retained was the distance in relation to the speaker, not the objectively oriented position in space. What we call a crossroads (four roads) the Latin sees as a *trivium* (three roads). We suspend ourselves above the space and see all four directions; the Roman does not see where he comes from. It can be maintained that the same thing appeared in art: while the Greek temple is made so one can go around it, the Roman temple is an opening set in an impenetrable background. While the Greek statue, since it is in rest, is made so one can view it from every angle, the Roman is on the march.[20] The Roman experience translates the same advance with respect to time, the same dislocation in relation to an origin. Hegel saw it well, even if he depreciated it: "From the beginning, Rome was something artificial, something violent, and not at all original" (*etwas Gemachtes, Gewaltsames, nichts Ursprüngliches*).[21] Now this situation is quite explicitly accepted. Unlike the Greeks for whom it was a point of honor not to owe anything to anyone, not to have had a master, the Romans readily admitted what they owed to others.[22] Unlike the Greeks who proudly claimed an autochthony that besides was obviously legendary,[23] the Romans related their origin to a non-autochthony, to a foundation, to transplantation into new soil.

---

20 H. Kähler, *The Art of Rome and her Empire* (New York: Crown, 1963), p. 27–34.

21 Hegel, *Philosophie der Geschichte, Gesammelte Werke*, ed. H. Glockner, vol. 11, p. 366, Glockner.

22. Cf. R. Harder, *Eigenart der Griechen. Eine kulturphysiognomische Skizze* (Freiburg-in-Breisgau: Herder, 1949), p. 36 ff.

23 Cf. N. Loraux, "L'autochtonie: une topique athénienne" in *Les enfants d'Athéna. Idées athéniennes sur la citoyenneté et la division des sexes* (Paris: Maspero, 1981), pp. 35–73.

The Roman relation to their origin, and the opposing
Greek relationship to theirs, stand out vividly in comparing
the two key words used to express them. These words are
without doubt untranslatable, but they are interesting in that
they reflect the differing senses all the more clearly as they
start from the same image, that of vegetable growth. Where
the Greek speaks of *physis* (from *phyein*), the Latin speaks of
auctoritas (from *augere*). The Greek *physis* ("nature") speaks of
what perdures, and expresses coming-into-being as a continuous[24] movement of unfolding out of a particular origin, and
as an installation in a permanence (the root *phy-* is that found
in the Latin *fui*, like "to be" in English). Conversely, the
Roman *auctoritas* ("authority") speaks of the fact of being the
author, the initiative that spans the gap that innovation created in relation to the ancient, and which guarantees or ratifies
the action of another as one's own.[25]

The myth of Romulus expresses just this sort of relationship to the origin: he founded what did not yet exist. The
genius of Virgil also seized and gave expression to just this
sort of relationship to their origin when he exploited the
Trojan legend and created in *The Aeneid* the Roman myth *par
excellence*. When Troy is sacked by the Greeks, Aeneas leaves
carrying with him his father and his domestic gods, ultimately transferring them to Latin soil. To be Roman is to experience the ancient as new and as something renewed by its
transplantation in new soil, a transplantation that makes the
old a principle of new developments. The experience of the
commencement as a (re)commencement is what it is to be
Roman.

---

24 Cf. my *Aristote et la question du monde. Essai sur le contexte cosmologique
    et anthropologique de l'ontologie* (Paris: Presses Universitaires de France,
    1988), p. 18 ff.

25 On this word, cf. R. Heinze, "Auctoritas" in *Vom Geiste des Römertums.
    Ausgewählte Aufsätze*, 3rd edition (Stuttgart: Teubner, 1960), pp. 43–58
    and E. Benveniste, *Vocabulaire des institutions indo-européennes*, vol. 2
    (Paris: Minuit, 1969), p. 150.

This experience was not limited to historical Rome. Nothing prevents one from recognizing its reflection in the medieval and renewed prolongation of Roman legend in European claims to a Trojan origin – and not only by the French.[26] Or consider how this theme, which is, besides, not exclusively European, is renewed in the tradition of the *translatio studiorum*, the liberal studies[27] passed from Greece to Rome and then, according to one's preference, to Florence or Paris.[28] Or finally, consider the American experience which is "Roman" in that it is founded on transplantation and on the idea of establishing a *novus ordo seclorum*, a desire that attests to the profoundly European legitimacy of the United States.

The Roman Attitude

My aim here is not to do history. Consequentially, it is even less to defend the historical reality of Roman imperialism which, let it be said in passing, has certainly not been the stupidest or cruelest that history has known. I will take the liberty of abstracting a "Roman attitude" from the givens of history. This attitude I will characterize in a general way as that of one who is conscious of a call to renew the ancient. Thus, for example, I will neglect the orators' ritual appeals to ancestral customs (*mos maiorum*). But, in return, I will support myself on a kernel of fact – that is, the Hellenization of Roman culture. This took place progressively, nearly from the moment that Rome came into contact with the Greek cities in southern Italy ("Magna Graecia," including Sicily), and continued at an accelerated rhythm from the Punic Wars on. This cultural borrowing had as a cause, as much as a consequence, a certain Roman feeling of inferiority toward the Greeks.

26 Cf. D. Hay, *op. cit.*, p. 48 ff. and 108 ff.

27 Literally, "the sciences" [*translator's note*].

28 Chrétien de Troyes, in his prologue to Cligès (1176), applies this schema to chivalry.

This complex of inferiority – even if one sought to mask it through diverse subterfuges – appeared first on the level of that universal support of culture, the language. The Latin language has never been particularly esteemed. From antiquity the Romans have always been conscious of the relative poverty of their language compared to the exuberance of Greek.[29] Admittedly, during the Middle Ages, Latin played the role of a universal instrument of communication for cultivated people. As such, it acquired some social prestige. But Latin remained characterized by a triple secondarity: a) it was no one's maternal language, but in every case a learned language before which everyone was equal;[30] b) it was not a specifically Christian language, but the language of a political rather than religious entity, an entity not Christian but anterior to Christianity, an entity that was even for a long time the enemy of Christianity: the Roman Empire; c) it was not the original language of Scripture, but that of a translation (the Vulgate) done from a Hebrew or Greek original. In the early modern period, Latin maintained a primacy in scientific communications, but this was for purely practical reasons.[31] Never was Latin considered to have exceptional privileges of a metaphysical order – for example, as being the absolute language.[32] The language of the first man was always thought to have been Hebrew, not Latin.

---

29   Cf. Lucretius, *De natura rerum* I, 139.832; III, 260; Cicero, *De finibus* III.ii.5; Seneca, *Letters to Lucilius* 58, 1; Pliny the Younger, *Letters* IV, 18; Saint Jerome, Letter 114 to Theophilus, Corpus Scriptorum Ecclesiasticorum Latinorum, 55, p. 395.

30   Cf. L. Bieler, "Das Mittellatein als Sprachproblem" in *Lexis* II, 1 (1949), pp. 98–105. This observation had already been made by Gibbon in his *Autobiography* (Oxford: Oxford University Press [World's Classics, no. 139]), p. 102.

31   Pascal, in the middle of the seventeenth century, still interrupted a mathematical demonstration begun in French with "and I will tell you that in Latin, since French is worthless" (letter to Fermat, July 29, 1654).

32   The idea that during the Middle Ages Latin had an absolute value is found in E. R. Curtius, *Europäische Literatur und lateinisches Mittelalter*

And later, one finds the same sense of disparity, even if the terms in which it played itself out had changed. Thus, the vernacular languages, confined first of all to minor literary genres, could develop into great literature only by proving their title to legitimacy in relationship to Latin.[33] Among the languages of modern Europe, one has still to insist, several centuries later, on the dignity of German compared to French, and of the Slavic languages in comparison to German, etc. But if they succeeded, it was because the languages in relation to which it was necessary to prevail, and Latin first of all, had not themselves the prestige of the preeminent language of culture: they were only some substitute for Greek whose past dignity had not been forgotten. Europe owes the linguistic diversification that has permitted its blossoming to the presence, at its source, of an original plurality. As an example of the opposite process, where Greek remained unchallenged, as was the case in the Byzantine world, the vernaculars, even Demotic Greek, could not attain the status of literary languages until very late.[34] Paradoxically, Demotic Greek attained a written form at a later date than even the Slavic languages whose speakers nevertheless entered into the space of Christendom well after the Greeks.

It is of little importance to recall here that the inferiority felt by the Romans of the second century was perhaps unjustified, as the Greeks of that period were hardly superior to their Roman contemporaries.[35] It is not a question here of objective facts which are, besides, quite difficult to measure; it is rather a matter of an impression of an affective order. The

(Bern: Francke, 1948), p. 33 – again cited in K. O. Apel, *Die Idee der Sprache in der humanistischen Tradition von Dante bis Vico*, 2nd edition, (Bonn: Bouvier, 1975), p. 91. This idea comes in fact from a misinterpretation of Isidore of Seville, *Etymologies* II 16, 2. The passage has besides been removed from the second edition of Curtius (1953).

33 Dante, *De vulgari eloquentia*.

34 Cf. H.-I. Marrou, *op. cit.*, p. 134.

35 Cf. P. Grimal, *Le siècle des Scipions. Rome et l'hellénisme au temps des guerres puniques* (Paris: Aubier, 1953), p. 13 ff.

important thing is that a disparity was felt and expressed. We find it, for example, in the hackneyed verse of Horace who said that "Captive Greece captivated the wild conqueror and introduced the arts into rustic Latium."[36]

This is seen still more clearly in the celebrated declaration that Virgil put into the mouth of Anchises addressing Aeneas, come to visit him in Hades. In an obviously retrospective prophecy, Aeneas's father gives advance justification for Roman imperialism in two celebrated verses. But before this, he begins by putting the art of government in its proper place:

> Excudent alii spirantia mollius aera
>
> (Credo equidem), vivos ducent de marmore vultus,
>
> Orabunt causas melius, caelique meatus
>
> Describent radio et surgentia sidera dicent.[37]

As one should not pretend to translate poetry, I will content myself with a paraphrase: others than the Romans – here, the Greeks – will be better sculptors, better orators, better astronomers; Rome will have to content itself with the profession of arms and with politics, with putting some order into a scene in which it will not be the protagonist.

The Aqueduct

Rome was not satisfied with administering the conquered world and bringing its own civilization to it. Rome equally, and even especially, brought a culture that did not come from it – the Greek culture. Péguy knew how to express this brilliantly:

> He [the Roman soldier] made not only the Roman and Latin worlds. Within, they bore the Greek world. That is, the first half of the ancient world. And ancient thought would not have been inserted into the world and it

---

36   Horace, *Epistles*, II, 1, 156.

37   Virgil, *Aeneid*, VI, 847–50.

would not have commanded the thought of the whole world if the Roman soldier had not proceeded to this temporal insertion, if the Roman soldier had not measured the earth, if the Roman world had not proceeded to make this sort of graft, unique in the world.[38]

Such comportment might not have won out. The Roman elites could have very well refused to Hellenize. The Roman model, the "Roman way,"[39] was not the only possible one. One can easily describe a counter-model, easily define the temptation that Rome resisted. It would have been easy for them to choose to preserve their "authenticity" intact, considered as a sign of primitive innocence, and to play it off against a refinement seen as a symptom of decadence. One can find in history examples of just such an attitude, for example, in the Slavophile movement of nineteenth century Russia. The Romans at least had the courage to bow down to Greek culture and to admit that they were a rough-hewn people, but nevertheless a people capable of learning.

In this sense, anyone is "Roman" who knows and feels himself caught between something like a "Hellenism" and something like a "barbarity." To be "Roman" is to have above one a classicism to imitate and below one a barbarity to subdue – though not as if one were only a neutral intermediary, a simple interpreter who is himself a stranger to what he communicates, but in knowing that one is oneself the scene in which everything takes place, in knowing oneself stretched between a classicism to assimilate and an inner barbarity.

To be "Roman" is to perceive oneself as Greek in relation to what is barbarous, but also as barbarous in relation to what

---

38 Péguy, "L'argent suite" in *Œuvres* en prose, 1909–1914 (Paris: Bibliothèque de la Pléiade, 1961), p. 1217. One should read the whole passage, pp. 1216–19; English in: Charles Péguy, *Basic Verities. Prose and Poetry*, rendered into English by Ann and Julian Green (New York: Pantheon, 1943), p. 161 f.

39 "La voie romaine" was the original title of the book in French [*translator's note*].

is Greek. It is to know that what one transmits does not come from oneself, and that one possesses it with difficulty, and only in a fragile and provisional manner.

Roman culture is thus essentially a passage: a way, or maybe an aqueduct[40] – another tangible sign of the Roman presence. This last image has besides an advantage over the image of a "way" in that it directly expresses the necessity of a disparity. While a roadway should be as flat as possible, an aqueduct is unthinkable without a slope. Similarly, Roman culture is stretched on an incline, between uphill and downhill.

Between "Hellenism" and "Barbarity"

What I call the Roman attitude is thus not proper to the image of the Romans given to us by history. It is also and first of all the fact of the Greeks themselves. They, or in any case the greater among them, considered themselves as former barbarians. The difference between Greek and barbarian was not one of nature, but purely of chronology: "The Greek world lived in a manner analogous to that of the barbarian world of today."[41] The Greeks are like heirs who have taken their goods from elsewhere, and this includes their gods.[42] It was perhaps even the feeling of a certain lack of originality, in every sense of this term, compared to the "old" river civilizations such as Egypt or Mesopotamia, that pushed them to rush toward what was new.[43] Greek life received the unrestrained rhythm that is its own: "The course of life in Greece

---

40   This superb image was suggested to me by B. Placido in a review of the first edition of the present work; cf. "Aridateci l'acqua corrente," *La Repubblica*, November 9, 1992.

41   Cf. Thucydides, I, 6, 6. Cf. also Plato, *Cratylus* 397c9–d2 and 421– d4 ff. as well as the implications of Aristotle, *Politics* II, 8, 1268b40.

42   Herodotus, *Inquiries* II.53.

43   Cf. the *Acts of the Apostles* 17:21, and Iamblichus, *De mysteriis Aegyptiorum* VII, 5, p. 259, 9–14.

was incredibly rapid."[44] And yet the Greeks distinguished themselves from the Romans on this capital point, that is, the absence of a feeling of inferiority compared to their sources. They had the impression of transforming what was received, and for the better: "everything the Greeks received from the barbarians, they ended up perfecting it every time."[45]

In any event, the same dynamic animates European history. One can characterize it from the point of view of the "Roman" attitude. This is the consciousness of having a Hellenism hanging above one, and beneath one a barbarity to subdue. It seems to me that it is this difference in potential between the uphill classical and the downhill barbarity that makes Europe advance.

The colonial adventure of Europe since the great discoveries, for example in Africa, has often been resented as a repetition of Roman colonization. An entire segment of French historiography has established a parallel between the colonization of the Maghreb by ancient Rome and the modern one accomplished by France, justifying the latter by the more ancient. In the same way, the colonizers identified themselves with the conquerors: "We . . . take up again, in improving on it, the work of the Romans."[46] One can, in a more penetrating manner, perhaps, push the parallel further and compare the European colonization of Africa with the Roman conquest of Europe.[47]

---

44 Cf. Schelling, *Einleitung in die Philosophie der Mythologie*, 16th lesson, p. 380.

45 Pseudo(?)-Plato, *Epinomis* 987d8–c2, and Origen, *Against Celsus* I, 2; *Sources chrétiennes* 132, p. 82.

46 E. Masqueray, *Formation des cités chez les populations sédentaires de l'Algérie: Kabyles du Djurdjura, Chaouia de l'Aourâs, Beni Mezâb* (thèse de lettres, Paris, 1886), reedited with an introduction by F. Colonna (Edisud [Archives maghrébines] 1983), p. 13. (Françoise Micheau provided me with this reference.)

47 The parallel is quite evident at the beginning of *Heart of Darkness* by Joseph Conrad.

One might wonder if the tie is not deeper yet, and if the avowed will to identify with ancient imperialism does not explain itself by a hidden desire for revenge on its predecessor. Could these two events, colonization and European humanism since the Italian Renaissance – contemporaneous on the scale of the history of civilizations – not be tied in a compensational relationship? One might venture to say that Europe's conquering ardor has long had, among its most secret mainsprings, the desire to compensate, through the domination of people it pretends are inferior, for its own feeling of inferiority in relation to classical antiquity – a feeling humanism always came along to revive. One might suspect that there is something like an equilibrium between the preponderance of classical studies and colonization: the school kids stuffed with Latin and Greek furnish excellent officers for the British Empire.[48] And, inversely, the end of the dominant role reserved to classical studies, in the post-war period, is contemporary with decolonization.

---

48   Cf. Kipling, *Stalky & C°*.

III

Religious Romanity:
Europe and Judaism

The situation of secondarity in relation to a previous culture, as we have just seen, constitutes what I call "Romanity." But this attitude can be illustrated just as easily from Greek texts. As a whole, it is anterior to Christianity, and therefore it left its mark on the Mediterranean independently of Christianity. In this context, what is the role of Christianity? It seems to me that Christendom and Europe owe it, of course not the existence, but the persistence of cultural secondariness. Indeed, if the attitude I call "Roman" is not the privilege of the Romans, there is another even more remarkable fact: it is not a privilege of the "pagan" or ancient side of European culture. It is just as assuredly the characteristic of its other side which, in order to avoid confusions that this term never ceases fomenting, I call not "Judeo-Christian" (how many problems stem from that hyphenated union![1]) but "Jewish *and* Christian."

I say therefore: the "Greek" and the "Jewish," inasmuch as they intervene as the two fundamental components of Europe, are both "Roman." More precisely, it is because Europe welcomes both the "Greek" and the "Jewish" compo-

---

1   A hyphen in French is literally a "trait d'union," a "line" or "feature" or "dash" of union; cf. also "trait d'esprit" [*translator's note*].

nents from a Roman point of view that these components can themselves remain and produce the plenitude of their effects. I will examine these two components successively: the "Jewish" one in the present chapter, the "Greek" in the one to follow.

The Two Senses of "Judaism"

One should ask oneself, then, about the relationship of Europe to its Jewish dimension. I must begin here by clearing up a possible misunderstanding by being a bit more precise. The adjective "Jewish" has indeed at least two senses that one must take care not to confuse. One may distinguish a wider and narrower meaning of "Jewish."

a) It can signify, in the wider sense, the whole of the Israelite people's experience, from its distant origins up to today. The founding events of this history have been selected and recorded in the writings of what the Jews call the Law, the Prophets, and the Writings (*TaNaKh*), and the Christians call the Old Testament. This history extends across the epochs of the redaction of the *Mishna*, then of the *Gemara*, in passing by the Middle Ages, and on to the emancipation and the modern epoch.

b) But the adjective also possesses a narrower meaning. It may also designate the Judaism that constituted itself after the destruction of the Temple in 70 AD and the fixation of the canon of Writings at Yavne some thirty years afterwards. In relation to this Judaism, the Christian Church is more in a relationship of fraternity, like a twin, one might say,[2] than of a descendant. As the New Testament illustrates well, from its nascent stages Christianity presented this relationship through an entire series of parables that presented a scene with two sons, one older and the other younger, the most celebrated being the one typically known by the name of the

---

2   A. Paul, in *Le judaïsme ancien et la Bible* (Desclée, 1987), speaks of "false twins."

"prodigal son" (Luke 15:11–32). These two sons are typically interpreted as representing, first, Israel, first object of the divine covenant, and second, the pagan nations, called later to join the covenant. On the Jewish side, one constantly meets with the not very flattering comparison of the Christians to Edom-Esau, the enemy brother of Jacob-Israel.

It is necessary, moreover, to distinguish between Judaism and the Jews. Not every Jew lives a Jewish life any more than every Christian or Muslim lives a Christian or Muslim life. I prefer here to reserve these adjectives for those who claim them, and then within the limits that they claim. In this way, one will avoid certain annexations forced *post mortem*, which besides would vary according to the preference of the interpreter. Of course, one can qualify a culture, an education, a cultural impregnation, a "sensibility" as Jewish or Christian, or even as Catholic or Protestant, etc. Nothing would prevent one from considering Spinoza Jewish in this sense. But one would then have to consider Voltaire as Catholic and Razi as Muslim as well. And, moreover, it would then be necessary to hypostatize a membership otherwise renounced by those one treats in this way, and to make a "Jewishness" that one would then be able to apply to whomever one wants, and even to those who do not want it.

Europe in Jewish History

In the narrow sense, the Jewish experience is not the privilege of Europe, nor even of Christendom. Jewish history has indeed taken place within the framework of European and Byzantine history, but just as equally within the Muslim world – and even beyond, extending to Malabar and to China. As to any judgment that one might make about this history, or about the question of what Europe has brought to Judaism, whether positive or negative, I would refer the reader to the historians, and above all to Jewish historians. The European course of Judaism is one of the stages of Jewish his-

tory after the exile, the dispersion, and then the destruction of
the Second Temple. It even represents one of the most negative stages as to the degree of submission to the Nations.
Indeed, the only experience of a nation converted to Judaism
occurred outside the framework of the Islamized or
Christianized Mediterranean: the kingdom of the Khazars, a
people living around the Crimea between the seventh and
eleventh centuries, whose elite converted to a Judaism that
was without doubt somewhat superficial.[3] And the case, an
exception, in which the Jews played the role of persecutor and
the Christians that of persecuted, took place a century before
Islam during the reign of *Dhu Nuwās* in sixth century
Yemen.[4] Everywhere else Judaism was, as the title of the
apologetic *masterpiece* of Judah ha-Levi, the *Kuzari*, has it, the
"despised religion" (*ad-dīn ad-dalīl*).[5]

This situation of humiliation applies to all of medieval
history in the whole Mediterranean basin. One can compare
the two shores, the Muslim and the Christian, from the point
of view of Jewish history. The comparison does not favor
Christendom. During the Middle Ages, the lands north of the
Mediterranean long remained, for those to the south, an
object of that stony contempt civilized societies show barbarians, and the Jews were no exception in this regard. Thus one
finds some remarks from the pen of Maimonides about the
filth of the cities located in the land of the "Franks," whose
similarity to contemporary stereotypes about the
Mediterranean world might elicit a smile:

3   Cf. D. M. Dunlop, *The History of the Jewish Khazars* (Princeton
    University Press, 1954), 293 pp.

4   *Encyclopaedia Judaica*, "Yûsuf 'As'ar Ya'thar Dhu Nuwâs" (H. Z.
    Hirschberg), vol. 16, col. 897–900, and J. Ryckmans, *La persécution des
    chrétiens himyarites au VIe siècle* (Istanbul: Nederlands historisch-
    archaeologisch instituut in het nabije oosten, 1956), 24 p.

5   Cf. also Saadia Gaon, *The Book of Beliefs and Opinions*, ed. Qafih
    (Jerusalem and New York, 1970), III, 10, p.148; English tr. S. Rosenblatt
    (New Haven: Yale University Press, 1948), p. 179.

> ... if swine were used for food, market places and even
> houses would have been dirtier than latrines, as may be
> seen at present in the country of the Franks.[6]

This unfavorable diagnosis is confirmed when one no longer compares their cultural level, but the situation of the Jewish communities. On the whole, and if one ignores some exceptions such as the persecutions of the Fatimid Caliph *Al-Ḥakīm* in Egypt, or that of the Almohads in Spain, the Jewish communities have in fact been better treated in the Muslim world than in the Christian one.[7] Modern Europe has been the framework of the largest massacre of Jews in history. Historians are still debating the question today whether modern anti-Semitism (called "scientific" from its foundation in a biological pseudo-theory), and in its wake the Nazi attempt to exterminate the Jewish people, are a continuation of the Christian (religious) anti-Judaism or represent a discontinuity in relation to it.

As to Christian anti-Judaism, there is considerable variation within it. The polemic of the Church Fathers against the Synagogue (for example in Saint John Chrysostom) most often remained verbal. But it prepared juridical measures: the legislation forbidding the Jews landed property and the exercise of certain trades goes back to the early Middle Ages. This legislation more generally fomented a distrust of the Jews that led in turn to explosions of violence which were, this time, quite physical.

And so Jewish history took, in the Orient as in the Occident, a particularly tragic turn. Central Europe, divided between the Orthodox and Uniate and Latin Catholics, was the theater of large massacres when the Cossacks revolted in

---

6   *Guide of the Perplexed*, III, 48; Joël, p. 439, 17 ff.; English translation S. Pines, (Chicago: The University of Chicago Press, 1963) p. 598.

7   Cf. L. Poliakov, "Musulmans, juifs et marranes" in *Les juifs et notre histoire* (Paris: Flammarion, 1973), pp. 34–75. In the same sense, cf. the more ample synthesis of B. Lewis, *Jews of Islam* (Princeton: Princeton University Press, 1984), XII–245 pp.

1648, and of sporadic pogroms until the beginning of our century. In the Occident, persecutions in the strict sense of the word (massacres, forced conversions, accusations of "ritual crimes," etc.) had hardly begun with the Crusades, but they continued at least until the expulsion from Spain (1492).

It is in part as a consequence of the hostility of the environment that Jewish history, in the contemporary period, tends to disassociate itself from European history. The centers of gravity of Jewish population in fact tended to be found less and less at the interior of the European space. The Jews have been leaving Europe, since the nineteenth century, toward America, and in the twentieth, toward Israel as well. This outflow has been compensated only very partially by the migration to France of Jews from North Africa after the latter's independence. And this tendency is likely to become generalized to the entire ancient continent with the exodus of Jews from the former Soviet Union. One can only wonder whether the European cycle of Jewish history is not on the point of concluding.

The Jewish Contribution to Europe

Conversely, the Jews as individuals have made their contribution to the two cultural spheres, in the south as well as to the north of the Mediterranean, and in multiple domains, from economy to religion in passing by politics and the sciences. As to medieval Europe, one fact played a capital role in the transmission of the classical intellectual heritage, once translated and commented on by Muslim thinkers, to Latin Christianity: the northern displacement, from Andalusia to Provence, of the intellectual centers of the Jewish Sephardic world beginning in the twelfth century. The Almohad persecution had pushed several topflight intellectuals (in particular, members of the Kimhi and Ibn Tibbon families) to take refuge in Christian Provence. There they translated what they considered the most important texts of thinkers of Arabic language, Jews or Muslims, into Hebrew.[8] Some of them owe their survival to this translation. Thus, for example, Themistius, whose commentaries on the *Treatise on the Heavens* and on book *Lambda* of the *Metaphysics*, both written in Greek, have survived in their entirety only in a Hebrew translation done from an Arabic original that is now either entirely lost or only fragmentary.[9] Similarly, nearly all the texts of Averroes exist in manuscript form in Hebrew, while the Arabic text of more than one is lost, as is the case, for example, of his commentary on the *Republic* of Plato.

A second stage of translation took place into Latin. Even where there was no Hebrew intermediary text, it happened that translations were made by teams in which a Jew played the principal role: he would translate the work from Arabic into one of the vernacular languages, which he would then dictate to a Christian cleric who in turn would record it in Latin.[10] Teams like this worked in the twelfth and thirteenth centuries in Toledo, and later in Naples. In this way, modern Europe owes a considerable debt to these Jewish translators. This impulse of translation coincided in fact with the European intellectual take-off that was linked to the foundation of universities, a take-off which the Jews perceived as

8   For this, the indispensable guide remains M. Steinschneider, *Die hebräischen Übersetzungen des Mittelalters und die Juden als Dolmetscher* (Graz, 1956 [Berlin, 1893]). Cf. also M. Zonta, *La filosofia antica nel Medioevo ebraico. Le traduzioni ebraiche medievali dei testi filosofici antichi* (Brescia: Paideia, 1996), 301 pp.

9   I have chosen this example as I have myself worked on this text. Cf. Thémistius, *Paraphrase au livre «Lambda» de la «Métaphysique»*, translated from the Hebrew and the Arabic (Paris: Vrin, 1999).

10   In respect of all this, one must pay homage to the works of Mlle. M.-T. d'Alverny, recently deceased (1991). Cf. in particular "Les traductions à deux interprètes, d'arabe en langue vernaculaire et de langue vernaculaire en latin," in *Les traductions et traducteurs au Moyen Age*, Actes du colloque international du CNRS (IRHT, 1989), pp. 193–201.

well as the others,[11] and in large part contributed to. But one wonders whether that contribution to European culture concerned Judaism as such.

One can ask oneself an analogous question with respect to the modern world. One can, of course, present good arguments establishing that in the last two centuries the Jewish experience has been decisive for European culture. But in this case it does not suffice to cite the names of Marx, Freud, Einstein, Kafka, and many others. One must consider to what extent these thinkers, and before all others, the authors of *The Jewish Question* and of *Moses and Monotheism*, are faithful representatives of Judaism, and to what extent their contribution to European culture, undeniable though it is, actually represents a contribution of Judaism as such. One would have to isolate an "essence" of Judaism. This operation is delicate for every religion; it is all the more so for Judaism which, properly speaking, has no "dogmas." In this order of ideas, one could thus, for example, attempt to show that the idea of law, even once uprooted from its original religious context – the Covenant – and formulated by confirmed unbelievers, continues to represent a common denominator for Jewish thinkers.[12]

However, whatever may be the response one chooses to give to these questions, Judaism as such has only been able to exercise an influence on European culture from a rather late

---

11 Cf. Samuel Ibn Tibbon, *Maamar Yiqqawu hammaim*, p. 175, ed. Presbourg, 1837, and later Crescas, *Or ha-Shem*, I, 10 (ed. of Ferrara, p. 256, 8 ff) and I. Abravanel, *Commentary on Joshua* 10, 12 (Jerusalem: Torah we-Da´ath, 1976), p. 53a. The same observation is found in Ibn Khaldun, *Muqaddima*, VI, 18, ed. Quatremère (I cite: Q), vol. 3, p. 93, 3–7; English translation, F. Rosenthal (I cite: R), Bollingen Series (University Press of Princeton, 1958), vol. 3, p. 117 ff.; For Byzantium, cf. F. Fuchs, "Die höheren Schulen von Konstantinopel im Mittelalter," *Byzantinisches Archiv* 8 (Leipzig, 1926), p. 66 ff.

12 H. U. von Balthasar, *Engagement with God*, tr. J. Halliburton (London: SPCK, 1975), pp. 71–76.

date. The Jewish communities have been excluded for a long time from any participation in political power that goes beyond the private role of certain of its members. In order for Judaism to be able to make itself understood publicly and get away from the confidential character imposed on its written productions by the exclusive use of Hebrew, one had to await the emancipation. This arrived in the eighteenth century, first in Germanic countries (Austria and Prussia), and then continued on in the wake of the French Revolution. During this period, Europe was already a cultural reality, and it was already conscious of its unity on this particular level. In this way, Judaism has been able to leave its mark, a decisive mark, on an already constituted Europe, but it has contributed only a little to *making* Europe.

Before the modern epoch, in fact, one can only note some minor exceptions, all found in intellectual domains. Thus, one can note the influence of Jewish exegetes on Christian exegesis: Origen and Saint Jerome used the skills of the Rabbis of their time, and the school of St-Victor used the commentary of Rashi. Even Luther, though known for pamphlets whose anti-Judaism went well beyond that accepted by his time,[13] often preferred to use the interpretations of David Kimhi in his translation of the Bible.[14] One will equally note the capital role played by Maimonides's *Guide of the Perplexed* in the formation of the great scholastics, and in particular of Saint Thomas Aquinas, who wrote in addition a *De regimine Judaeorum*.[15] Outside of these dialogues between scholars, the single case of influence of any scope and of a popular nature is repre-

---

13   On the regressive features in the work of Luther, cf. K. Flasch, *Das philosophische Denken des Mittelalters von Augustin zu Machiavelli* (Stuttgart: Reclam, 1987), pp. 587–89.

14   Cf. the synthesis of G. Dahan, *Les intellectuels chrétiens et les Juifs au Moyen Age* (Paris: Cerf, 1990), pp. 289–307.

15   Other than the works of W. Kluxen, cf. A. Wohlman, *Thomas d'Aquin et Maïmonide. Un dialogue exemplaire* (Paris: Cerf, 1988), 417 pp.

sented by Spain, which remained an exception.[16] All of these phenomena, thus, continued to be somewhat marginal.

The Contribution of Ancient Israel

On the other hand, the Biblical experience expressed in the Old Testament has obviously contributed greatly to make Europe what it is. And since this influence was exercised before all else through the intermediary of Christianity, I shall consider it from this perspective. One remark, however: Christianity received the Old Testament in a very different way than Judaism. The latter recapitulated the experience of the Old Covenant by taking the Torah as its sole principle. Christianity, on the other hand, preserved some elements that Judaism had left aside or reserved for Messianic times: the sacrificial dimension of the Covenant lost its pertinence for Judaism after the destruction of the Second Temple; it survived in the Christian sacraments. Davidic royalty had disappeared under foreign domination; it resurged in the sacerdotal mission of the Christian emperors and the kings of the west. Prophecy had disappeared, and Judaism had taken notice of this disappearance, which it explained in diverse ways; in Christianity, it continued in the role of the Saints, and in particular, with the founders of orders. One may choose to interpret these analogies either as the survival of archaic characteristics or, on the contrary, as the salvation of the whole of Revelation at the price of its "spiritual" reinterpretation.

Following my practice in my treatment of Greece and Rome, I will not attempt a detailed inventory of what Europe has inherited from ancient Israel. In such a case, it would be necessary to distinguish several styles of reception, according to whether one was speaking of the Catholic, Orthodox, or Protestant world. The way in which the Bible is present differs in each of these three domains, as does the accent placed

---

16 A. Castro, *España en su historia. Cristianos, moros y judios* (Barcelona: Critica, 1984; first ed., 1948), ch. X, pp. 447–555.

on the two halves of it. I will therefore concern myself here, once again, less with the content transmitted than with the form of that transmission, and with what made that transmission possible.

If one did want to concern oneself with the content, the list of the Old Testament's cultural influences on Europe could, in a sense, be very quickly drawn up, and it has been many times. But it includes such enormous entries that I could not reproduce it without taking up the entire European tradition in detail, and there is no question of doing this here. For example, we would have to examine in detail the idea of the supremacy of man over the rest of creation, and in particular, over the animals which were supposedly created for him. Or again, the idea that man's relation to God is realized especially through moral practices came to Europe from the prophets of the Old Covenant. Or finally, the idea of a temporality that is radically non-cyclical, given an absolute beginning (the Creation), and maybe an end, is obviously Biblical in origin.

One may note, in this regard, outside the very negative image that historical Rome has left on Israel,[17] a parallel between this linear representation of time and the Roman experience of temporality: as some have already observed, Aeneas, the Roman hero par excellence – and just the opposite of Ulysses, who ends up recovering his hearth – may be the best pagan parallel to Abraham's leaving his lands, his fatherland, and the house of his father.[18] Similarly, one can put in parallel the foundation of Rome and the non-autochthony of the Hebrews, who know quite well that, on entering Canaan, they inhabit houses that they have not built and harvest the fruits of trees that they did not plant.[19]

---

17   Cf. the synthesis of M. Hadas-Lebel, *Jérusalem contre Rome* (Paris: Cerf, 1990), 553 pp.

18   Cf. Th. Haecker, *Vergil, Vater des Abendlandes* (Munich, 1952), pp. 109–12.

19   Cf. Joshua 24:13 and Deuteronomy 6:10 ff. For the context, cf. my essay

The Secondarity of Christianity

If ancient Israel has some "Roman" characteristics, what can we say about Christianity? To begin with, we can satisfy our-selves with recalling a few obvious points. They are valid of the Church before the schisms of the Orient and the Occident, and later of the Reformation, and for the Catholic Church, which is called "Roman." This title, as everyone admits, is more than a historical or geographical contingency. It is so completely obvious that the Church is the heir of the Roman Empire, that one sees in it either a sign of election or of repro-bation. But here, I will not concern myself with what content might have passed from historical Rome to the Church, for better or worse. I will only consider the form of the Roman attitude, which does not depend on the maintenance of such content, and which can therefore survive it.

I set down therefore as a thesis that this "Roman" structure is the very structure of the Christian reality. The Christians are essentially "Romans" in that they have their "Greeks" to which they are tied by an indivisible bond. Our Greeks are the Jews. To say it a little less quickly: Christianity is to the Old Covenant what the Romans were to the Greeks. The Christians know – even if they are constantly in danger of for-getting, as they have done on several occasions – that they are grafted onto the Jewish people and onto their experience of God. That is to say, the covenant is connatural with the Jewish people since the covenant constitutes it as such: a total sepa-ration from the covenant would be to stop being a part of this people. On the other hand, for the Christians, the covenant is something that must be learned. It is in this sense that the existence of Christians in the covenant is "against nature." As Saint Paul does not hesitate to say, the Christians have been grafted on the Jewish people "against nature" (*para physin*) (Romans 11:24). This is why their models of relation to the

---

"L'expérience biblique du monde et l'idée de création" in *Création et salut* (Bruxelles, 1989), pp. 105–20, and especially p. 111 ff.

truth are different: the Jewish model is the wisdom by which an original gift arrives at its blossoming; the Christian model is culture, the implantation of what a primitive nature had not received in the beginning.[20]

The Church is "Roman" because it repeats the operation carried out by the Romans in regard to Hellenism, but in relation to Israel. This structure of the Church is what makes the continued presence of the Jewish people necessary and prohibits any attempt to consider what they have brought as something relegated to a completed past. This structure is also what makes it recapitulate what appeared then as "ancient," beginning with what it confesses as its principle. The Church is "Roman" because it is founded, and because it is founded on the Christ that it confesses to be novelty itself. In a celebrated text, Saint Irenaeus dared to say that Christ brought nothing new, but that he brought everything as if new:

> He brought all [possible] novelty by bringing Himself [omnem novitatem attulit semetipsum afferens] who had been announced. For this very thing was proclaimed beforehand, that a novelty should come to renew and quicken mankind.[21]

He brought nothing new in that he did not come to add something to what preceded; he brought everything new in that he is the principle of everything, "the principle who speaks to you," as the Vulgate has it in an ingenious mistranslation of John 8:25.

The Relation to the Old Testament

The relation to the experience of the Old Covenant occurs, necessarily, in relation to the writings where the moments

---

20 Cf. E. Peterson, "Kirche aus Juden und Heiden" (1933) in *Theologische Traktate* (Munich: Kösel, 1951), p. 281.

21 Irenaeus, *Against Heresies* IV, 34, 1; *The Ante-Nicene Fathers* (Grand Rapids: Eerdmans, 1953), vol. 1, p. 511b.

have been recorded that are considered decisive in its turbulent history. These texts form what we have the habit of calling the "Old Testament." This terminology is, as one knows,
of Christian origin. Also of Christian origin is the habit of
associating two groups of texts in one single book – the Book
– that is, the Bible. One of the two is determined by the other
in the most profound sense. The New Covenant and the New
Testament which constitutes its documentation are so inti-
mately related to the Old Covenant and the Old Testament
that they draw on them for everything up to and including
their name. The adjective "old," which qualifies the covenant
and the texts that record it, does not signify "lapsed" or
"superseded." It refers to a chronological and logical priority
of such a sort that it would be better to speak of the "first"
Testament.

If this is the case, it is first of all because the Old Testament
of the Christian Bible essentially coincides with the writings
recognized as canonical by Judaism. The Christians add, as is
known, a certain number of texts: the two books of
Maccabees, the Wisdom of Ben Sira (Ecclesiasticus), Tobit,
Judith, Wisdom, and Baruch. All these have their roots in
Palestinian, Babylonian, or Alexandrine Judaism. Several
have existed in Hebrew (Wisdom of Ben Sira) or in Aramaic
(1 Maccabees). The admission of several has been debated by
the rabbis. It does not seem that their exclusion, on the Jewish
side, was motivated by a desire to thwart Christianity. Nor
does it seem, on the Christian side, that their addition was
part of a willful attempt to distinguish themselves from a
Jewish canon that was already fixed. Moreover, this was not
yet the case. It seems that the two canons established themselves in parallel, that a single magma flow crystallized in
two independent ways which remained quite near to one
another on the deepest level.

Afterwards, the presence of those texts in the same corpus
that was accepted as authoritative shows that the two collec-
tions were set on the same level. This situation is not self-evi-

dent. The relationship of Christianity to the Old Covenant was indeed a source of constant tension, and even of ruptures, or in any event of conflicts. It would be much easier to pretend that the Old Covenant has purely and simply lapsed and is now replaced by the New. This radical solution was defended for the first time in the second century by Marcion: he proposed abandoning the writings of the Old Testament, which supposedly reflected only an angry God, which would be now superseded by the New Testament, though expurgated, the work of a God of love. It may be that Marcion was applying to exegesis here the Gnostic practice of separating a bad creator of inferior rank from a supreme God who is both good and outside the world, and from whom Christ came as His messenger. The temptation of Marcionism remained a constant problem for the Church. It turns up again with the Cathars, if one can consider them as Christian, and extends all the way to certain marginal tendencies of liberal Protestantism as, for example, found in Harnack:

> The rejection of the Old Testament in the second century was an error that the Great Church rejected quite rightly; preserving it in the sixteenth century was a fate that the Reformation had not yet the force to evade; but preserving it as a canonical document within Protestantism since the nineteenth century is the consequence of a weakening of the religion and of the Church.[22]

In addition, one has been able to locate its influence up to and including certain contemporary sensibilities.[23]

---

22 A. von Harnack, *Marcion: das Evangelium vom fremden Gott. Eine Monographie zur Grundlegung der katholischen Kirche* (Leipzig: Hinrichs, 1921), p. 248 ff. Harnack points to Tolstoy and Gorky as contemporary resurgences of Marcionism.

23 E. Bloch in *Geist der Utopie* (1918) explicitly claims to follow Marcion. M. Buber saw the danger of Marcionism for Judaism. Cf. "The Spirit of Israel and the World of Today" (1939), *On Judaism*, Edited by N. N. Glatzer (New York: Schocken Books, 1967), p. 187 ff. For a diagnosis of Marcionism applied to other cultural phenomena, cf. A. Besançon, *La*

But this temptation was always exorcised in the last instance. From the beginning, the Church recognized the validity of the words of Christ according to which there is no question of abolishing the old Law, but of fulfilling it to perfection (Matthew 5:17), the words of Saint Paul, according to whom the promises of God to Israel are without repentance (Romans 11:29), the words of Saint John, who has Christ say that "salvation comes from the Jews" (John 4:22). Later, the Fathers of the Church – particularly Justin, Tertullian, and Irenaeus of Lyon – would also resist this same temptation. Tertullian insisted on the verse of Matthew just cited, one that Marcion eliminated from his version of the New Testament.[24] Irenaeus expressed the essential point in a concise formula:

> Both the Mosaic law and the grace of the new covenant,
> as both fitted for the times [at which they were given],
> were bestowed by one and the same God for the benefit
> of the human race . . . God . . . is one and the same . . .
> who was announced by the law and the prophets, whom
> Christ confessed as His Father.[25]

Such a position was more acrobatic than the one which declared either that the ancient Revelation was purely and simply lapsed or that its essential content was no better preserved than in the new one – in such a way that the old appeared as an empty shell, ready to be disposed of. This attitude was held, heroically, because the interpretation of the Old Testament can be delicate, and even troubling for the Church. Indeed, the Old Testament does not refer so clearly to the New; and the words of Christ, according to which the mission addresses itself first of all to Israel (Matthew 15: 24), risk putting in doubt the legitimacy of the mission on which

---

confusion des langues. La crise idéologique de l'Eglise (Calmann-Lévy, 1978), esp. ch. VI, "Gnose, idéologie, marcionisme," pp. 133–63.

24 Cf. Tertullian, *Adversus Marcionem*, ed. and trans. E. Evans (Oxford: Clarendon Press, 1972), IV, 7, p. 278 ff.

25 Irenaeus, *Against Heresies*, III, 12, 11; *The Ante-Nicene Fathers, loc. cit.*, p. 434b and IV, 5, 1; p. 466b.

the Church is built, the mission to the pagans. On the other hand, on the Jewish side, it would be tempting to try to push Christianity toward Marcionism so as to avoid a kinship that has proved dangerous and which remains compromising. This is why one must salute the courage, parallel to that of the Fathers, with which certain Jews, notably Franz Rosenzweig, have dissuaded the Church from separating itself from the Old Covenant and from everything it represents.[26]

Islam and the Preceding Books

The comparison with Islam here is very instructive. Islam places itself in continuity with, first, the Jewish tradition, then with the Christian. As is known, the Koran cites numerous figures of the Old Covenant, for example, Adam, Noah, Abraham, Joseph, Moses, and certain prophets such as Jonas. With regard to the New Testament, the Koran names the greatest of all the prophets (excepting Mohammed), that is to say Jesus, to whom it gives the title of "Messiah," and says that he was born of a virgin. One has no trouble noticing some borrowing from the Jewish oral tradition or from the Christian apocrypha in certain more or less marvelous details. But in the Koran, in any event, these personages are cut off from the economy of salvation that gives them meaning for Jews and Christians. Thus, to speak only of the New Testament, Jesus is certainly called "Messiah," but without any relation to the Jewish messianic idea as the fulfillment of history. Mary is called a virgin, but without the significance represented through the miraculous birth of Jesus in breaking the continuity of generations, that is, the entry into the world of a new mode of historicity. And Jesus is presented without his death on the cross and resurrection, which make, one might say, all his interest . . .

In a general way, Islam, especially the Sunni version, does

26 Cf. *Der Stern der Erlösung*, III, 3 (Frankfurt: Suhrkamp, 1990), pp. 461 ff.

not recognize the idea of a "history of salvation."[27] All the
messengers of God, in the Old Covenant as outside of it –
even the prophets sent to the disappeared peoples – preach
only a single message, and it is that which appears in its
definitive purity with Mohammed. The series of their por-
traits forms a typology that repeats itself: warning, rejection
of the prophet, punishment of the guilty people. Only in a
marginal way does one recognize the idea of an alliance of
God with his people, and this alliance is never as clear as
when it occurs before history, in the scene of the pre-eternal
pact (*mīṯāq*) when Allah demands that future generations,
drawn simultaneously from the loins of Adam, attest that he
is indeed their Lord.[28] In no case is there a question of God
engaging himself in the human adventure.[29]

This is the case because Islam does not accept the Writings
that locate the Biblical personages in an economy of salvation.
Admittedly, Islam reveres what it calls the "Torah." It reveres
what it calls the "Evangel" – in the singular. The prophet of
Islam says explicitly to "confirm" the preaching of the previous prophets. But he understands by that, not the texts, but
the authentic message that they would contain. And this message, according to Islam, is not that which one can read in the
texts of the Pentateuch and of the four Gospels we possess.
Indeed there exists in Islam an entire tradition founded on the
Koran (IV, 46) that accuses Jews and Christians of having
altered the text of the Writings that had been entrusted to
them.[30] The theologians do not agree exactly on the nature of

---

27   Cf. some luminous pages of A. Falaturi, himself a Shiite Muslim, in
     "Das Fehlen einer Heilsgeschichte im Islam," *Miscellanea Medievalia* 11,
     "Die Mächte des Guten und Bosen" (1977), pp. 72–80.

28   Cf. Koran, VII, 172.

29   See the very keen analysis in R. Arnaldez, *Trois messagers pour un seul
     Dieu*, 2nd ed. (Paris: Albin Michel, 1991), ch. I, in particular pp. 19–26.

30   Cf. *The First Encyclopaedia of Islam*, "Taḥrīf," vol. 7, col. 618b–619b (Fr.
     Buhl). As often happens, the first modern author to have discussed the
     case is I. Goldziher, in "Über muhammedanische Polemik gegen Ahl
     al-Kitâb" in *Gesammelte Schriften* (Hildesheim: Olms, 1968), vol. 2, pp.

the phenomenon: for some the texts have simply been badly interpreted; but the dominant theory is that they have been knowingly modified. Thus one finds authorities who forbid the study of any revealed text other than the Koran. One supports these findings, of course, on the statements of the Prophet. Notably, he said to the future Caliph Omar whom he had found reading a page of the Pentateuch, that the Koran sufficed.[31]

This attitude of principle has had a consequence that history is a witness to: the texts of the Old and New Testament are in fact read in the Islamic world only exceptionally. The examples of direct consultation of Jewish or Christian sources, as with Ibn Qutayba, remain rare.[32] Even Al-Ghazâlî (if the text is his) who, in criticizing the Christians, has the honesty to base himself on the Evangels, cites them according to Muslim sources.[33]

All these usages are found at the interior of fundamentally critical undertakings. Sometimes this was a matter of showing that the religious communities who claimed a text as source did not themselves really understand it – in which Islam approaches the Christian polemic against Judaism – and sometimes it was a matter of showing that the texts had

---

1–47. The most complete presentation that I know of is Mgr. Ignazio di Matteo, "Il '*tahrîf*' od alterazione della Bibbia secondo i musulmani," *Bessarione* 26 (1922), pp. 64–111 and 223–60; cf. also W. Montgomery Watt, "The Early Development of the Muslim Attitude to the Bible," *Glasgow University Oriental Society. Transactions* 16 (1955–56), pp. 50–62; H. Lazarus-Yafeh, *Intertwined Worlds: Medieval Islam and Bible Criticism* (Princeton: Princeton University Press, 1992), xiii–178 p. See also some good lines in J. Chabbi, *Le Seigneur des tribus. L'islam de Mahomet* (Paris: Noêsis, 1997), pp. 57–61.

31   Ibn Khaldun, *Muqaddima* VI, 9; Q, vol. 2, p. 387, 10–13; R, vol. 2, pp. 438 ff.; One finds the same story in Attar, *Le livre divin*, French trans. F. Rouhani (Paris: Albin Michel, 1990 [1961]), V, pp. 138 ff.

32   Cf. G. Lecomte, "Les citations de l'Ancien et du Nouveau Testament dans l'oeuvre d'Ibn Qutayba," *Arabica* 1958, pp. 34–46.

33   Cf. al-Ghazâlî, *Réfutation excellente de la divinité de Jésus-Christ d'après les Evangiles*, text established, translated, and annotated by R. Chidiac, S.J. (Leroux, 1939), pp. 32 f.

been corrupted by bringing to light the contradictions and even absurdities they contained. The most remarkable of these attempts was perhaps that of the Spaniard, Ibn Hazm (994–1064). He introduced some methods of Biblical criticism that can be found, even if one can only with difficulty demonstrate his influence, in the age of Enlightenment. In any event, he throws an almost Voltairian light on the Old and New Testament.[34] And it is remarkable that he shows his surprise before the fact that the Christians accept the Old Testament.

Christianity and the Texts of the Old Covenant

Whereas the accusation of a foundation on corrupt, and therefore unusable, texts remains the basis of the Muslim attitude toward the Biblical religions, a similar accusation is, in contrast, only very exceptional on the part of the Christians toward the Jews. The presence of a common scriptural basis is recognized by the two parties, even in the most vivid of polemics. The Christians know that they can base themselves on the Old Testament in order to argue with the Jews. The highest authorities on both sides have recognized this. Thus, in Christianity, Thomas Aquinas argues:

> Some, such as the Muhammedans (*Mahumetistae*) and the pagans, do not agree with us about the authority of any writing by which they could be convinced, as we can dispute against the Jews with the Old Testament.[35]

Or among the Jews, Maimonides:

---

34 The passages of the *Fisâl* are accessible in Spanish in a lightly "Christianized" translation of M. Asin Palacios, *Abenhazam de Cordoba y su historia critica de las ideas religiosas* (Madrid: Revista de archivos, bibliotecas y museos), vol. 2 (1928), pp. 238–392; and vol. 3 (1929), pp. 9–118. Cf. R. Arnaldez, *Grammaire et théologie chez Ibn Hazm de Cordoue* (Paris: Vrin, 1956), pp. 309 ff.

35 Saint Thomas Aquinas, *Summa contra Gentiles*, I, 2. Cf. also Saint Bonaventure, *On the Hexameron*, XIX, 14, p. 124; Duns Scotus, *Ordinatio*, prologue, §99.

The uncircumcised [the Christians] are convinced that the text of the Torah is just the same.[36]

This is why, where a difficult controversy arises between the Church and the Synagogue, it is about what interpretation to give to the Old Testament, and not about its authenticity.[37] It even happens that the Jewish texts posterior to Christ (posterior, that is, with regard to at least their definitive editing), such as the Talmud, and even the texts of the Kabbala, have been the objects of a Christian attempt at allegorical interpretation with a view to seeing there the announcement of Jesus. Islam, on the other hand, was never interested, as it seems, in the Talmud.

This difference of attitude between Christianity and Islam is, perhaps, so to speak, prior to the birth of the latter, and a fact which helps to explain it. Among the causes of the success of Mohammed's preaching was in fact the inferiority complex of the Arabs with respect to the Jews: unlike the Jews, they had no holy book. It was the refusal to consider himself as being without a book, and therefore as "ignorant," it was the desire to rise from "ignorance" (*jāhiliyya*) that caused the hope for an Arab prophet and an Arab kerygma (*koran*), and that made people welcome them when they presented themselves.[38] Christianity, on the other hand (and especially in its Pauline version become orthodox, and not in the Judeo-Christianity that, on this level at least, has perhaps prepared the terrain for a nascent Islam[39]) presupposes the

---

36   *Responsum*, no. 149, in *Teshuboth ha-Rambam . . .*, ed. Y. Blau (Jerusalem: Meqitsey Nirdamim, 1958), vol. 1, p. 285. For some exceptions, cf. I. M. Resnick, "The Falsification of Scripture in Medieval Christian and Jewish Polemics," *Medieval Encounters* 2 (1996), pp. 344–80.

37   Exceptions: the discussions on the canon in Dahan, *op. cit.* p. 444 ff., and one text: *regnavit a ligno Deus* which the *Vexilla Regis* attributes to David (maybe Psalm 95:10).

38   M. Rodinson, *Mahomet*, 3rd ed. (Paris: Seuil, 1974), p. 126 and *passim*.

39   Cf. S. Pines, "Jahiliyya and 'ilm" in *Jerusalem Studies in Arabic and Islam* 13 (1990), pp. 175–94.

acceptation of an inferiority complex in relation to Judaism, a true circumcision of the heart.

One should be careful, therefore, not to make an implicit analogy between what one calls, with an expression that besides is quite superficial, the "three monotheisms." Islam is not to Christianity (not even to Christianity and to Judaism) what Christianity is to Judaism. Admittedly, in both cases, the mother religion rejects the legitimacy of the daughter religion. And in both cases the daughter religion turned on its mother religion. But on the level of principles, the attitude toward the mother religion is not the same. While Islam rejects the authenticity of the documents on which Judaism and Christianity are founded, Christianity, in the worst case, recognizes at least that the Jews are the faithful guardians of a text that it considers as sacred as the text which is properly its own. In this way, the relationship of secondarity toward a preceding religion is found between Christianity and Judaism and between these two alone.

IV
Cultural Romanity: Europe and Hellenism

According to my view, the relation of Europe to its sources is essentially "roman." I have tried to show it in relation to its Jewish source. I must now attempt the same demonstration for its Greek source. One will see how this "roman" attitude is present even in the humblest and most material aspects of the transmission of ancient heritage. Here, I will treat principally the transmission of philosophical texts.

The ancient world, as in general all that is past, is not known to us directly, but only through traces. Sometimes these are mere vestigial remains, such as found in buildings. Most often they are found in written texts. We seem to have a direct access to these texts, as it suffices to read them. Admittedly, this "suffices" does not mean that it will be easy. On the contrary, we know well that a whole battery of preparations are in order: we must learn their language, prepare to understand them by becoming familiar with the world that witnessed their birth, learn to read them as their authors wanted to be read – for example, by provisionally accepting the conventions of the literary genre to which they belong. But despite all these precautions, the fact remains: we have these texts; they are at our disposal.

One must learn to see, behind this manifestly present object, an invisible whole that precedes it and which may be thought of as its foundation. I mean their very transmission in its diverse modes: copying, translating, and adapting.[1] Each of these modes will be illustrated successively through one of the three worlds: the Greek, the Arab, and the Roman.

The Greeks: Copying

The literary works that we have conserved from Antiquity are the result of a work of selection. The channels that have transmitted them to us have equally functioned as filters that did not let just anything pass through, and this filtering took place from Antiquity on. One must then avoid a way of seeing things, which I believe erroneous and which has been encouraged by the fact that we ourselves speak of "the" Greeks and "the" Romans. We are tempted to understand these as two entities, two simple and homogeneous groups. But one must realize that each of these groups contains a mass, a mass that was sometimes considerable.

One must make a habit of keeping a chronology of world history before one's eyes. I remember the astonishment of my students in the first course of the history of philosophy I taught at the University of Dijon. On the blackboard, I drew them a chronological table on a scale of some 4 to 8 inches per century. One sees then the enormous place taken by the Greeks. When did philosophy begin? It emerged progressively, because there was already considerable thought, for example, in Hesiod. We may place Thales, the first in the collection of pre-Socratic philosophers, toward the beginning of the sixth century before our era. When did Greek philosophy end? First, has it ended? The teaching of philosophy was not interrupted in Byzantium. But for the sake of argument, let's

---

1 I leave out here the givens of the "auxiliary sciences" for which I refer the reader to the excellent collective work *Die Textüberlieferung der antiken Literatur und der Bibel* (Munich: dtv, 1975), 623 p.

say that it had a provisional end with the closing of the school of Athens in 529, and with its last master Damascius, during the period of the last neo-Platonic commentators on Aristotle – Simplicius, a pagan, and John Philoponus, a Christian. If, therefore, one observes that Greek philosophy extends from Thales to Damascius, one realizes that it covers a period of roughly twelve centuries. That is, the same period that separates us from Charlemagne.

To say "the" Greeks then is already heavy-handed. Could we imagine speaking of a single entity as "German philosophy," extending from Meister Eckhart in the thirteenth century to Heidegger or Wittgenstein? This would already be an excessive simplification, though the time covered is approximately half of that covered by Greek philosophy.

Now, during this period of more than a millennium, the transmission of Greek heritage began. It began between Greeks. The first intermediaries between the Greeks and us were . . . the Greeks themselves. But this transmission did take place, and first of all, it did not *always* take place. The Greek heritage was not always transmitted by the Greeks themselves. Why? Because the texts were not for the Ancients what they are for us.

The Trouble of Conservation

This arose in part out of the mode of transmission. Antiquity had not yet entered the "Gutenberg galaxy" dear to McLuhan. That is, a text was only transmitted to posterity once it was copied. For us, once a text is printed, it is more or less saved: numerous copies are distributed and protected in libraries. To conserve it, it suffices simply to conserve it. A purely negative decision suffices: don't throw it out; don't destroy it. One is familiar with the problems that have begun to arise for modern librarians: the overly acidic paper used in recent times promises a shorter life-span to printed matter than was the case with the medium used for ancient writings.

Whatever solution one might offer to this problem – the transfer to computerized media, for example – its mere existence
bears witness to a fact: for us, the ideal relation to written arti-
facts is a book that conserves itself.

For us, the conservation of works is not an arduous
process; it was, however, before the printing press, the fruit of
a conscious decision and a constant effort. We let texts sleep
in libraries; for the Ancients, it was necessary to lend them a
hand. Only exceptionally were texts preserved in a medium
as durable as stone. The case of Diogenes of Oenoanda is
famous in this regard. This Asiatic of the second century of
our era had a résumé of the Epicurean philosophy he adhered
to engraved on the wall of a portico. The building was
destroyed, but the stones were reused, leaving a puzzle for
the erudite to reconstruct.

But the immense majority of texts were entrusted to
papyrus, or later, to parchment, both fairly fragile media.
Thus, to conserve a work, one had to make a conscious choice
to have it recopied once its material support had deteriorat-
ed.[2] This was a tedious and costly enterprise that one hesitated to undertake. It could only be done for a limited number
of copies, and not for just any work. All of this goes to explain
a well-known fact: the literature of antiquity has survived
only in a very fragmentary way.

Destruction?

One often explains this fragmentary survival by means of
destruction, voluntary or otherwise. The scenes of this black
legend inflame the imagination. And all the more so to the
extent that one holds accountable, not just the stupidity of the
barbarians, such as that of the Vandals whose name has

---

2   See the beautiful example in Themistius, *Orationes* IV, 59b–61d and the
    analysis in P. Lemerle, *Le premier humanisme byzantin. Notes et remarques
    sur enseignement et culture à Byzance des origines au Xe siècle* (Paris:
    Presses Universitaires de France, 1971), p. 56.

become proverbial, but also recognizes the force of a willful obscurantism – in which case one thinks of the infamous burning of the library of Alexandria.[3]

It is true that book burning is a very ancient practice, as witnessed by ancient writers going back to Periclean Athens and Imperial Rome.[4] It is also quite true that different families of thought didn't hesitate to suppress the writings of their competitors. And this was as true of philosophical schools as of religious groups. Among philosophers, we might even think of Plato, who supposedly wished to see the works of his rival Democritus burned.[5] And among religions, the successive Christian destructions of heretical works at the end of Antiquity or the burned Talmuds of the Middle Ages come to mind. As to Judaism, one can take, as an example, the first polemic of 1233 about the works of Maimonides and the way his adversaries got the Dominicans to bring about their destruction through fire. In Islam, we think of the Sunni tradition (though not entirely certain) about the destruction of exemplars of the Koran before the text was fixed by the Caliph 'Uthman, or about that of the Encyclopaedia of the "Sincere Brethren," that was suspected of Ismailism.[6]

---

3   The legend seems to come from Ibn al-Qiftī, *Ta' rīḥ al-ḥukamā'*, p. 355 ff., ed. J. Lippert. Gibbon seemed to have already contested it, *The History of the Decline and Fall of the Roman Empire*, ed. Bury, LI, vol. 5, pp. 452–55. Cf. P. Casanova, "L'incendie de la bibliothèque d'Alexandrie par les Arabes" in *Académie des Inscriptions et Belles-Lettres. Comptes rendus. . .* , 1923, pp. 163–71. One finds an analogous story about Omar, related to the Persian books of the Magian, in Ibn Khaldun, *Muqaddima*, VI, 18; Q, vol. 3, p. 89, 20–90, 5; R, vol. 3, p. 114.

4   Cf. Protagoras, DK 80 A 1 (Diogenes Laertius, IX, 52), 3, 4. On Rome, cf. A. Momigliano, *Problèmes d'historiographie ancienne et moderne* (Paris: Gallimard, 1983), p. 65.

5   Aristoxenos, fg. 131 Wehrli (Diogenes Laertius), IX, 40; Marinos, *Life of Proclus*, ch. XXXVIII ff.

6   Other examples may be found in F. Micheau, "Au Proche-Orient, les parfums du savoir" in *La bibliothèque: miroir de l'âme, miroir du monde, Autrement* 121 (April, 1991), p. 52 ff.

But one must think of this vision of things, which is either too tragic or too romantic, in relative terms. The principal cause of the loss of ancient literature is negative – that is, the non-recopying of works. And non-recopying is not the mark of a positive will of destruction.

Outdated

It can indicate, first, that certain texts are considered as outdated, and as uselessly occupying papyrus or parchment, rare and costly media, which one was tempted to scrape clean and reuse. Such texts were lost particularly because they no longer seemed to reflect the truth one believed had been attained at a certain stage of research. Thus, certain passages have disappeared, not because they were purely and simply suppressed, but because the work they figured in was reviewed, adapted to a new stage of knowledge, and therefore corrected. This was especially true of manuals transmitting scientific or technical knowledge. Take, for example, works of medicine. The historian of medical knowledge would like to possess the original version of the text he is studying. But the manual he has in his hands was not written for historians, but for the practitioner who, at his patient's bedside, desired to have the surest guide possible. In such works, why would one leave assumptions known to be outmoded and that would lead one to err? In such a case there was less a desire to destroy than to correct.

Even among the actual destructions whose memory has been transmitted to us, many occurred less out of a consciousness of danger than of outdated material. If the Ephesians burned books of magic, it was because the miracles of Saint Paul had displayed, not their malice, but their uselessness (Acts 19:19). And on this point, the Ancients did in a sense exactly what we do with a certain category of texts. Consider schoolbooks. Do we conserve physics textbooks when the program has changed, or the précis of constitutional history after the fall of an old regime? Think about what it means when a bookseller "just can't use" certain titles.

The non-recopying of a work can also be related, not to the work itself, but to the reader. A text is recopied only in order to be read. But one must be able to find readers capable of understanding it. So it happens that simple résumés and compendiums, no doubt less remarkable, but more didactic and accessible – and, since they are shorter, less expensive to have translated and copied – are substituted for richer and more developed works. One should not be surprised, then, that the Muslim world seems to have backed away from translating the two long political dialogues of Plato, or the highly abstruse *Timaeus*, and preferred Galen's résumés to the originals.

Whatever the cause of a text not being recopied, its effect was definitive. We can exhume forgotten authors because we possess them in printed form and have only to withdraw them from the forgotten shadows of the library where they sleep. This was not the case in the ancient world. Woe be, then, during those times, on to all texts that no longer attracted the attention of their contemporaries, since they no longer corresponded to their intellectual and spiritual needs! They purely and simply disappeared.[7] Only what the transmitter judged pertinent and interesting was transmitted to us. This was sometimes what he esteemed the greatest success in the production of a writer. This was also sometimes what he considered as most susceptible of containing a truth, a truth that could be taught in a course, that is to say, most often, in a commentary.

The Struggle for Survival

We do not have a strong enough sense of the "struggle for life" which resulted in the selection of ancient works. For us,

7   See, for example, the remarks of Seneca, *Natural Questions*, VII, xxxii, 2, p. 335, Oltramare and the Emperor Julian, *Letter to a Priest*, 301cd.

a work of little interest is condemned to dusty shelves, whence a later generation can always retrieve it. For the Ancients, a work that had stopped being interesting for a somewhat long period was condemned to death without appeal, unless saved by an extremely improbable chance – the rediscovery of a papyrus in the sands of Egypt, or in the wrappings of a mummy, or smothered by ashes at Pompeii, or finally, miraculously traced on the floor, like that scrap of a philosophical dialogue, perhaps of Aristotle, recently discovered in Afghanistan.[8] One can certainly say, "We may not possess all of them, but at least we possess the masterpieces." Maybe – but who selected them? And in function of what criteria? It's one thing to put together an "ideal library" privately when one can draw on a real library, another to decide which work will survive and which will be left out. It is not a question of knowing, as the well-known mundane question puts it, "what would you take to a desert island," but rather of knowing, to continue the metaphor, who would have the right to get on the raft. . . . It's what lends a bitter taste to the anthologies put together by ancient literary critics:[9] their *krisis*, their judgment, was one of life or death.

One can grasp this fact better from a few examples. Thus, we owe the possibility of speaking of Parmenides to almost one individual: Simplicius, who decided to recopy large extracts of the Eleatic philosopher's poem in his commentary on Aristotle's *Physics*. And he recopied it, as he says in a very moving passage, because the book was rare.[10] Without him, we would have less than half of what we now possess of

---

8   Cf. P. Hadot and C. Rapin, "Les textes littéraires grecs de la trésorerie d' Aï Khanoum," *Bulletin de correspondance hellénique* CXI (1987), pp. 225–66, esp. 232–49.

9   Cf. the authors of the recommended reading list put together by Quintilian, XI, 1, 37 ff.

10 Simplicius, *In Aristotelis «Physicorum» libros [. . .] commentaria*, ed. H. Diels (Commentaria in Aristotelem graeca, IX) (Berlin: 1882), p. 144, 28.

Parmenides's poem, and in particular, would lack fragment VIII, which is of capital importance. Similarly, if we can speak of Epicurus, we owe it especially to Diogenes Laërtius, who had the bright idea of citing in their entirety three "letters" (in fact, treatises), which summarize his doctrine. But other thinkers have been less fortunate.

One can take Stoicism as an example. As one knows, we possess, in its entirety, none of the works dating from the beginning of this school. We must content ourselves with brief fragments that have often come down to us indirectly by way of citation. What is more, their closeness to the original and the sympathy of the one citing the text, and so his effort of comprehension, are often inversely related. Thus, Diogenes Laërtius speaks fairly honestly of the Stoic system, but he does it by means of a doxographical manual that is fairly flat. On the other hand, Plutarch may cite some fragments of Cleanthes or Chrysippus verbatim, but it is only to show, through supporting texts, how absurd their doctrine was. Why was it like this? Because as a school, Stoicism ceased to exist fairly early on. It seems to have disappeared around 260 of our era with a certain Kallietes, of whom we know almost nothing, except that he appears to have been the last scholarch. Stoic philosophy ceased being taught in the midst of a solid organization. From that point on, one had no need of manuals or of texts to comment on. And as the demand for such works dried up, so did the need to recopy them.

Aristotelianism had more luck, thanks to a fertile misinterpretation of it by the Neo-Platonism that remained alone in the lists at the end of Antiquity. The Neo-Platonists considered the Aristotelian writings (Aristotle himself, and his commentators not yet tainted with Neo-Platonism, like Alexander of Aphrodisias or Themistius) as having a propaedeutic value in logic and in physics, as a stepping stone toward a Neo-Platonic metaphysics.

Epicureanism and Stoicism, however, could not enter into the Neo-Platonic synthesis. Thus, they saw close before their eyes the doors of the conceptual Noah's Ark that could have saved them. The only properly Stoic works to have survived were those that had a moral value. Indeed, for ancient philosophy, morality has always constituted the grounds of kind of sacred union that neutralized technical rivalries between schools.[11] Similarly with late Antiquity: in the first century, the Stoic Seneca, in his *Letters to Lucilius*, cites and comments on some sentences of Epicurus with praise; in the third century, Porphyry draws on Epicurean arguments for support;[12] in the sixth century, the Neo-Platonist Simplicius writes a commentary on the *Manual* of Epictetus,[13] etc.

And so, the text that we have in our hands, with a few rare exceptions, is the result of a work of selection carried out by past generations. This selection took place according to certain criteria. And these criteria were, of course, those of the people of Antiquity. And they were not our own. Yet less did they take place according to atemporal criteria that would determine the eternal value of a work. Our knowledge of the ancients is, as with any historical knowledge, essentially mutilated.[14] Let us take care, therefore, to avoid thinking that we see Antiquity in its just proportions. We see it as the late Greeks decided to preserve it.

The Arabs: Translating

The Greeks, the Romans, and us, of course. But there are also the Greeks, the Romans, and the others. In particular, there is this world that Christendom has long considered as its

---

11 Cf. my *Aristote et la question du monde, op. cit.*, p. 58.

12 Porphyry, *On Abstinence*, I, 49–55; in I, 7–12, he cites Hermarchus to criticize him.

13 Simplicius, *Commentaire sur le «Manuel» d'Epictète*, intro. and critical ed. of the Greek text by I. Hadot (Leyden: Brill, 1996), 476 pp.

14 P. Veyne, *Comment on écrit l'histoire* (Paris: Seuil, 1971), pp. 24 ff.

"other" *par excellence,* and which it has not arrived at under-standing completely, that is, the Muslim world. The passage through the Arab world can help us become aware of several interesting facts and see what strangeness is hidden behind the evidence through which we see ourselves.

It was pointed out above that the Muslim world has also, after its fashion, been the heir of Antiquity, and as such it is a completely legitimate heir.[15] In this world, the transmission of the Greek heritage took place as a consequence of a deliberate decision aimed at resolving a problem that was very con-sciously perceived: the Muslim conquerors, on leaving Arabia and moving up toward Syria and Mesopotamia, found them-selves in a world that, though admittedly not without provin-cial characteristics, was culturally Hellenized. There they dis-covered a richness of knowledge and of know-how that had to be appropriated.

Now, there are several ways of appropriating the literary legacy of the past. Translation is not the only way. For exam-ple, the Roman world, both ancient and medieval, did not conceive of the appropriation of its past heritage through the mode of translation, but through another way which I will return to.

The cultural world that conceived and practiced a rela-tionship to the Ancient world through translation was partic-ularly the Muslim world. The great translators were not the Romans of Antiquity or of the Middle Ages; they were the Arabs. I use the terms "Arab" and "Muslim world" cautious-ly, without pretending to identify the two adjectives: not every Muslim is an Arab, nor is every Arab Muslim. But translation occurred particularly into the language of the cul-ture practiced by all Muslims, whether Arab, Persian, or Turk, and practiced also by those who lived in the Muslim cultural sphere, whether Jewish or Christian, or even belonging to the

---

15   Cf. *supra,* ch. 1, p. 15 f.

small pagan sect tolerated as a result of subterfuge, the Sabaeans whose elites were perhaps the direct heirs of the last Neo-Platonists of Antiquity.[16]

Was this translation the result of a conscious policy, formed at the highest level? One has spoken a great deal of the politics of translation practiced by the Caliphs. I will therefore limit myself to the essential points, and will add a few nuances.[17] A legend has formed in relation to this which recounts that the Caliph Al-Ma'mûm had a dream in which he saw Aristotle appear before him answering his questions. This dream, then, moved him to send ambassadors to Byzantine territory charged with procuring Greek manu-scripts.[18] One often speaks of the celebrated "House of Wisdom" in Baghdad that, from around 830, supposedly sup-ported a team of translators by trade, paid at public expense. In fact, the further one goes back in time, the less one finds a relation between the House and the activity of the great trans-lators. In the ancient sources, "the great translators are never mentioned in relation to the Bayt al-hikma,"[19] and this insti-tution no doubt had a role less focused on the diffusion of profane knowledge than on religious propaganda, in the con-text of the support lent by the Caliphs to the "theologians" of Mutazilite tendencies.

---

16   Cf. Michel Tardieu, "Sabiens coraniques et sabiens de Harran," *Journal asiatique* CCLXXIV (1986), pp. 1–44.

17   I have learned and borrowed a great deal from M.-G. Balty-Guesdon, "Le Bayt al-hikmah de Baghdad," *Arabica* XXIX (1992), pp. 131–50.

18   Cf. Ibn al-Nadîm, *Fihrist*, VII, 1, English trans. B. Dodge (New York: Columbia, 1970), vol. 2, p. 583 ff. and Ibn Abi Oseibia *'Uyūn al-anbā fi ṭabaqāt al-aṭibbā'*, "Hunain ibn Ishaq," ed. Dar Maktabat al-Hayat (Beirut, n.d.), p. 259 ff.

19   M.-G. Balty-Guesdon, *op. cit.*, p. 137 and D. Gutas, *Greek Thought, Arabic Culture: The Graeco-Arabic Translation Movement in Baghdad and Early 'Abbāsid Society (2nd–4th/8th–10th Centuries)* (London and New York: Routledge, 1998), pp. 54–59.

Whatever the institutional base of the enterprise of translation, the translators in any case existed: their works prove as much. But who were they? Some personalities stand out, as is the case with the dynasty of Hunayn ibn Ishaq, father, son, and nephew.[20] The translators were often Christian. In any event, the further one goes back in time, the more this appears to be the case. Why? Because Christianity, in its diverse variants, was the common religion of the Middle East before the Islamic religion established itself. And because it already existed prior to the Islamic conquest, an entire movement of translation from Greek to Syriac had developed which it only served to continue. The translators were thus the heirs of Greek knowledge, though Christianized in Syriac schools.

This vast movement of translation lasted little more than a century, as it began around the middle of the eighth century, and seems to have ceased by the eleventh. In this period, the Arab world ceased translating and would take up this practice again only under the shock of confrontation with modern Europe. One has to ask, what were the reasons behind this lapse? Certainly, and even if the movement seems to have stopped before the beginning of the (relative) decline or stagnation of Islamic civilization, these reasons are not without a relation to the more general causes which explain that decline. They are of different orders: economic, political, ideological (and particularly juridical), etc. As to how to decide which of these one should emphasize, the question remains open. I would thus refer the reader to the historians.[21]

---

20 Cf. the recent synthesis of M. Salama-Carr, *La traduction à l'époque abbasside. L'école de Hunayn ibn Ishâq et son importance pour la traduction* (Paris: Didier, 1990), 122 pp.

21 Besides the general works, see a first synthesis in R. Brunschvig and G. E. von Grunebaum, eds., *Classicisme et déclin culturel dans l'histoire de l'islam*, Actes du symposium international d'histoire de la civilisation musulmane (Bordeaux, June 25–29, 1956) (Paris: Besson-Chantemerle, 1957), 396 pp.

It will be sufficient there to touch lightly upon certain reasons of an intellectual order that contributed to this stagnation.

The Transmitted Content

Translation was done starting from Greek, but not uniquely. There also one must enlarge the perspective to include other worlds besides the Ancient Mediterranean one. The Arabs also translated from Middle Persian (Pahlavi) and from the languages of India. This took place in medicine, for example, but also in other domains, including spirituality, and as a part of this, yoga.[22] The first great translator, Ibn al-Muqaffa, presented an exemplary Arabic version of *Kalila and Dimna*, a collection of Persian tales, itself of Indian origin, and thus made accessible the masterpiece that inspired fabulists all over the world, La Fontaine first among them. One might also note the extraordinary migration of *Barlaam and Joasaph*, which started out among the stories on the life of Buddha and became nearly unrecognizable as a great "bestseller" of the medieval world.[23]

Because of its central geographical position, the Muslim world played the role of interpreter between Orient and Occident, in the economic as well as in the cultural sphere. One can apply the theory of Maurice Lombard on the economy of the Islamic world to the cultural domain. By installing itself as a wedge between the Occident and the Orient, Islam facilitated communication between these separate worlds. According to this view, on the one hand, it intercepted, to its profit, East-West commerce; and on the other hand, by recirculating fossilized riches, gold frozen in icons or on sar-

---

22 Cf. S. Pines and T. Gelblum, "Al-Biruni's Arabic Version of Patanjali's Yogasutra," *Bulletin of the School of Oriental and African Studies* 29 (1966), pp. 302–25, 40 (1977), pp. 522–49, 46 (1983), pp. 258–404, etc.

23 Cf. the article of T. Bräm in R. Goulet, ed., *Dictionnaire des philosophes antiques*, vol 2 (Paris: CNRS, 1994), pp. 63–83.

cophagi, it injected new blood into world commerce.[24] And in the cultural domain, it played an analogous role of intermediary.

Despite this, to return to the center of our subject, the effort of translation brought, above all, knowledge from the West. Whereas it seems that only one Latin text was brought into Arabic, the *Historiarum adversus paganos libri VII* of Paulus Orosius,[25] the mass of what was translated was of Greek origin.[26] Yet these were not always from Greek *texts*. There were indeed intermediaries even more invisible than those I have already named, the Persian world, for example. It seems that certain texts of Greek origin, though not numerous, particularly agricultural or astronomical texts, entered into the Arabic language through translations done into Medieval Persian.[27] The most important intermediary, however, was the Syriac cultural world.[28] Syriac had become the language of culture and communication of the Christian Orient. Many things already existed in this language, and it was the maternal language of a good number of translators.

What did they translate? Perhaps because they followed the habits of Syriac-speaking Christians,[29] very little of what

---

24   M. Lombard, *L'islam dans sa première grandeur* (Paris: Flammarion, 1971).

25   Cf. G. Levi Della Vida, "La traduzione araba delle storie di Orosio," *Al-Andalûs* 19 (1954), pp. 257–93.

26   Here again, the essential guide is the work of M. Steinschneider, *Die arabischen Übersetzungen aus dem Griechischen* (Graz, 1960) (a reedited version from works that appeared between 1889 and 1896).

27   Cf. C. A. Nallino, "Tracce di opere greche giunte agli Arabi per trafila pehlevica," *Raccolta di scritti editi e inediti*, vol. VI (Rome: Instituto per l'Oriente, 1948), pp. 285–303.

28   See the recent synthesis of G. Troupeau, "Le rôle des syriaques dans la transmission et l'exploitation du patrimoine philosophique et scientifique grec," *Arabica* XXXVIII (1991), pp. 1–10.

29   Cf. R. Paret, *Der Islam und das griechische Bildungsgut* (Tübingen: Mohr, 1950), p. 15 ff.

we would call "literature" was translated.[30] Certain themes passed from the Greek novel to the Arabic tale,[31] but on the whole the Arabs translated hardly any history, no epic or lyric poetry, and in particular, no tragic or comic theater. This is perhaps one of the reasons for the remarkable absence of this literary genre from the great Arabic literature of the classical period – with the exceptions of the theater of popular shadow plays, which originated in China, and the Shi'ite celebration of the death of Husayn in certain types of "mysteries."[32] On the other hand, the Arabs translated a great deal of mathematics and astronomy, a great deal of medicine, and even of alchemy. In all, an enormous quantity of books in science and philosophy.[33] So enormous in fact that, quite often, the Arabic translation is the only trace left of works of philosophy, mathematics, or astronomy whose originals we have lost.

I have said that the Arabs translated, indeed, translated a great deal. This means, on the one hand, that they transmitted to the Occident the Greek heritage in every domain:[34] medicine,[35] mathematics, philosophy, and this to such a point that

---

30   Cf. G. Wiet, "Les traducteurs arabes et la poésie grecque," in *Mélanges offerts au P. René Mouterde* . . . Mélanges de l'Université Saint-Joseph, Beyrouth, XXXVIII (1962), pp. 361–68.

31   Cf. G. E. von Grunebaum, *Medieval Islam. A Study in Cultural Orientation.* (Chicago: University of Chicago Press, 1946), ch. IX, "Creative Borrowing: Greece in the Arabian Nights," pp. 294–319.

32   For an explanation that takes greater account of the religious context, cf. G. E. von Grunebaum, *Islam: Essays in the Nature and Growth of a Cultural Tradition* (London: Routledge & Kegan Paul, 1961), p. 99.

33   Cf. the anthology of texts translated in F. Rosenthal, *Das Fortleben der Antike im Islam* (Zurich: Artemis, 1965).

34   The bibliography is immense. One can orient oneself thanks to the very equitable and serene panorama presented by W. Montgomery Watt, *The Influence of Islam on Medieval Europe* (Islamic Surveys, 9) (Edinburgh University Press, 1972), 125 pp., as well as to J. Schacht and C. E. Bosworth, eds., *The Legacy of Islam*, 2nd ed. (Oxford: Clarendon Press, 1974), 530 pp.

35   We note the recent work of D. Jacquart and F. Micheau, *La médecine arabe et l'Occident médiéval* (Paris: Maisonneuve et Larose, 1990), 271 pp.

philosophy especially owes an enormous cultural debt to the Arab world. This debt was still recognized (in all the senses of the word "recognition") in the Middle Ages by Gerbert of Aurillac, Roger Bacon, Frederick II of Sicily, though sometimes not without an occasional feeling of inferiority as found in Albert the Great, who wrote in regards to the theory of intellect: "in this domain, as in many others, I abhor everything that the Latin writers maintain."[36] The admiration for the treasure of reflection and of knowledge of Arabic provenance did not however prevent a vigorous polemic over doctrine. Thus, though he cites with equal force Greek, Arabic, and Latin writers, Saint Thomas is hard on Averroes: "who was less a peripatetic than a corrupter (*depravator*) of the peripatetic philosophy."[37] Duns Scotus, on the other hand, does not hesitate to draw on Avicenna.[38]

Whatever may be the case, recalling the importance of the Arabic translations does not mean to say in any event that the Arabs would have been satisfied to transmit books passively whose content was sealed off from them. Entirely to the contrary; they have equally been creators. They extended, sometimes by a great deal, the knowledge they received. In mathematics, for example, they brought about some decisive advances, well beyond what they received from the Greeks.[39] In astronomy, the school of Maragha took a decisive step in

---

36 *De Anima*, III, 2, c. 1, l. 59–60; ed. C. Stroick, *Opera omnia*, t. vii–i, 1968, p. 177b. Cited by A. de Libera, *Penser au Moyen Âge* (Paris: Seuil, 1991), p. 111.

37 *De unitate intellectus*, 2, *Opuscula Philosophica*, ed. R. Spiazzi (Turin: Marietti, 1954), §214, p. 76a and 5, §265, p. 89b.

38 Cf. the seminal article by E. Gilson, "Avicenne et le point de départ de Duns Scot," *Archives d'histoire doctrinale et littéraire du Moyen âge*, 1927, esp. p. 187.

39 Cf. the work of R. Rashed, in particular *Entre arithmétique et algèbre. Recherches sur l'histoire des mathématiques arabes* (Paris, 1984), p. 7 ff. with appendix, "La notion de science occidentale," pp. 301–18.

the critique of the Ptolemaic system, a step in the direction of Copernicus, who perhaps knew certain of the results.[40]

In philosophy, it is more difficult to evaluate the originality of the thinkers in the Arabic language. There are several reasons for this. First, one basic reason is that the notion of progress means something completely different in philosophy than in the scientific domain. Secondly, because one often has some difficulty in discerning what is creative and what is simply an adaptation of Greek works that have disappeared. For example, it has been debated to what extent Al-Farabi was original or only set out for us some lost Hellenistic work.[41] Finally, because every philosophy draws from its sources and because one can always give oneself over to the vain exercise of saying that one or another thought is "already" present in one or another precursor. But in this case, Occidental philosophy is all just as little original as that of the Muslim Orient. And thus we would have no more reason to say, for example, that Avicenna's ontology comes from Neo-Platonism than we would for Thomas Aquinas's.

The Romans: Adapting

To speak of the Romans after the Arabs seems not only contrary to good sense, but also to chronology. The Romans began to concern themselves with the Greeks several centuries before the Arabs ever entered on the scene. And yet, their work furnished, not only in the context of the present work, but also with respect to actual history, a transition

---

40 See the recent synthesis in G. Saliba, "The Astronomical Tradition of Maragha: A Historical Survey and Prospects for Future Research," *Arabic Sciences and Philosophy* (1991), pp. 67–99.

41 Thus, R. Walzer suspected that there must be a lost Hellenistic treatise behind almost every text of Al-Farabi. Farabi should no doubt be credited with greater independence. Cf. M. Mahdi, "Al-Fârâbi's Imperfect State" (on Walzer's edition of *The Ideal City*), *Journal of the American Oriental Society*, 110.4 (1990), pp. 691–726.

toward our own modernity. We are and remain, in particular for the Arab world, "rumis" – inhabitants of "Rumelia," and therefore, Romans.[42] And by "Roman" I understand, above all, the world of the Latin language – which lasted, among those who think and write, until well after the Middle Ages.

In the Middle Ages, these "Romans" themselves also recopied a great deal. To tell the truth, they recopied nearly the whole of what we possess of ancient literature. The enormous labor of the monks, and of the Benedictines in particular, must be mentioned here. There also one finds a conscious policy. To protect against the dangers of destruction from invasion, Cassiodorus founded around 540 the convent of Vivarium, whose task it was to protect the classical texts. Pope Gregory the Great followed his example some forty years later when he welcomed the monks who had just been chased from Mount Cassino and confided the same task to them, which they continued to carry out for more than a thousand years.

As to translation, when all is said and done, the Romans did little. They adapted, rewrote, and rethought the texts in transposing them into their own cultural world. In Antiquity, they were more inspired by Greek models than translators of them. There are multiple examples: Lucretius versified Epicurus; Cicero summarized the manuals of the middle Academy, all the while replacing the edifying stories which illustrated them with anecdotes of great Romans; Horace transposed Alcaeus; Virgil competed with Homer. But as to actual translators, excepting "technical translations" (agricultural manuals, etc.), there were very few down to a relatively late period: in the fourth century, Marius Victorinus translated some excerpts of Plotinus; Boethius, executed in 524 – five years before the closing of the school of Athens – had begun

---

42 *Rumelia* (*Rumeli*) was the Turkish name for the European part of the Ottoman Empire in the Balkans, including parts of ancient Macedonia and Thrace. [*translator's note*.]

to translate Aristotle. In the Middle Ages that followed, the situation was hardly any better, and for a very simple reason, that is, the enormous decline in the knowledge of Greek. Even among the rare thinkers who knew it, the tradition of free adaptation continued. Translation and adaptation form two parallel currents, sometimes even for the same person. Thus, John Scotus Eriugena (who died around 880), following the wave of translations of Dionysius the Areopagite by Hilduin (832–835), not only translated the Greek Fathers (thus, Gregory of Nyssa or Maximus the Confessor), but also drew very liberally from them to compose his own works.

If the Romans of the high Middle Ages translated Aristotle, it was on the heels of the Arabs and sometimes starting from Arabic translations. This occurred especially in Spain, land of confrontation and encounter with the Islamic world, and particularly in Toledo, where numerous translators were active in the second half of the twelfth century. In parallel, translators began to work directly from Greek, as we find in the example of William of Moerbeke's translations that were used by St. Thomas Aquinas. The manuscripts then used came from the Byzantine world. Later, direct contact with Greek culture was reestablished when Byzantine scholars immigrated to Italy after the fall of Constantinople.

I stop here to note that the activity of translation underwent a decisive transformation in the Middle Ages that gave it the appearance it has preserved up to our time. Between the eleventh and twelfth centuries, translation was separated out from paraphrases that rewrote the original, and began to strive for the ideal of as literal a rendering as possible, doing no more than transposing the sense into another language. The model that guided translators and placed them all, explicitly or not, "under the invocation of Saint Jerome," was the Biblical text.[43] Now this text was endowed with authority, an authority it could not maintain unless it was maintained in

---

43   Cf. Zonta, *op. cit.* ch. III, p. 89 ff.

its letter, or translated as closely as possible. Thus, the status of the sacred book determined the model of cultural transmission that remained in practice in Europe. I will show later on other consequences of this status.

Recognition and Denegation

The reestablishment of direct contact with Byzantine Hellenism brought about a cultural short-circuit: one could jump over the Arabic intermediaries. In an analogous fashion, and only a little later, the same phenomenon reoccurred in the domain of material civilization: the plans of Henry the Navigator (died 1460) resulted in the voyage of Vasco da Gama (1498), permitting one to reach the Orient in bypassing the Islamized world. Everything was in place to allow the development of a systematic and global denegation of Arabic heritage.

This was especially the case starting with the humanists who, as good Ciceronians, poked fun at the bad Latin of the translators of Averroes – and of the scholastics themselves. The conscience of a debt remained clear, however, for the great orientalists of the seventeenth century – Postel, Pococke, or Fontialis. But it was repressed from memory during the Age of Enlightenment, and again in the nineteenth century. In Germany, Mommsen spoke of the Islamic world as the "executioner of Hellenism."[44] In France, Renan was sadly distinguished in this domain, in particular, in his lecture of 1883, "Islamism and Science," which led to an interesting dialogue with El-Afghâni. He maintained that Greece was the unique source of knowledge and wisdom, and presupposed a teleological interpretation of history according to which it was necessary for Arabic science to disappear once Europe was inoculated with the ancient heritage. Finally, he added to the "enlightened" prejudice a racism that began by seeking out a

---

44 *Histoire romaine* VIII, 2, 12 (1885), French trans. Laffont, collection Bouquins, vol. 2, p. 927b.

biological foundation, explaining away all the innovations he had to concede to the Islamized world by means of the Persian, and therefore "Aryan," origin of the thinkers that world had produced.[45] One might mention in passing that the Occident has been repaid with the same sort of debased coin by those proffering the delusion, in inverted exaggeration, that the Arabs invented everything.[46]

Let us underline one characteristic of this polemic. It accepts that some of the cultural goods it prides itself on were received from others. But there are others – and then *others*. Certain "others" are more distinguished than others. In consequence, they will accept being indebted to the former, but on the other hand, will conceal transmitters that are no longer acceptable. For modern Europe, Byzantium was an honorable origin, but the Islamic world had ceased to be one. Thus, one made the Renaissance (itself considered as a unique event) begin at the moment when the Arabic intermediary became useless, relegating the preceding period, during which it was indispensable, to the supposedly dark ages. And the more colonization came to confirm the small interest of the Arab world, the more the Renaissance assumed the role of a glorious and decisive break.

It is interesting to note that the same vision of things, *mutatis mutandis*, was found in the Arab world during the preceding stage of our history. The same play was performed, but with different actors. The Arab world had a tendency to devalue the Greek world contemporaneous to it, that is, the Byzantine intermediary, to the profit of the original Greek one, that of pagan antiquity. The more time went on, the more the Arabic historians presented the transmission of the manuscripts of the philosophers and scholars of antiquity as having occurred, not through Byzantium but, one might say, over a Byzantium supposed to have been hostile to their content.

---

45 *Œuvres complètes*, vol. 1 (Paris: Calmann-Lévy, 1947), pp. 945–60.

46 Cf. the typical work of S. Hunke, *Allahs Sonne über dem Abendland: unser arabisches Erbe* (Frankfurt: Fischer, 1965), 358 pp.

Thus one arrived at the extremely revealing account by the fifteenth century author, Suyuti (1445–1505):

> the king of the *Rūm* [the Romans of Byzantium] fearing that their subjects would abandon the Christian religion after reading these works, had the books of philosophy walled up. When *Yaḥyā ibn Ḫālid ibn Barmak* asked for them, he jumped for joy, convened the bishops, the patricians, and the monks, and proposed to send the books without asking that they be returned.[47]

The facts are improbable, in particular because there are somewhat more efficient ways for getting rid of troublesome books than to build some sort of blockhouse around them. But the account remains quite interesting: for the author, who was attacking philosophy, it was a matter of spreading a dangerous poison among his enemies. The structure remained the same for those who defended it, whether it was to refute it or simply to understand it: the transmitters were incapable of appropriating what they transmitted. In the same order of ideas, I would even be tempted to consider, as a hypothesis, that the tales about the califs' ambassadors who were sent to procure manuscripts in the Byzantine territory were, if not invented, at least "inflated" because of concerns of this sort. A good number of the manuscripts containing the ancient heritage had no need to be imported from Byzantium. They were already in Islamic territory, either in Greek or Syriac, in the monastic libraries of the Christians. Their guardians were tributaries, subjects of inferior estate, and to admit to being indebted to them was unpleasant. . . . It was therefore more honorable to extrapolate from facts that were perhaps real enough, and to imagine that the Greek heritage passed, in its totality, directly from the capital of the emperors to that of the caliphs.

---

47 I found this text, and several of my ideas, in the article of M.-G. Balty-Guesdon, *op. cit.*, p. 136. This author himself depended on indirect citations that I have not been able to verify. I prefer, therefore, to cite the paraphrase of the author; see Gutas *op. cit.*, pp. 83–95.

A Continuous History

In this history, one searches in vain for an absolute source, whatever it might be. The exercise is as puerile, whether the result is positive or negative, as when children on a playground[48] set out to discover "who started it." One must first of all disassociate the question of priority from that of influence. A good example is provided by the problem of the origins of courtly love. As is well known, its themes, the submission of the lover to a lady become nearly divine, and the exasperation of desire through lack of satisfaction, appeared in the countries of *langue d'oc* starting with Guillaume IX of Toulouse. They were found as well, however, several centuries earlier in pre-Islamic Arabia as a poetic convention ("odhrite" love). Courtly love remained, in Baghdad of the ninth century as in Andalusia of the eleventh, a subject of debate for a long time afterwards. The anteriority of Arabic "courtoisie" is undeniable. But the hypothesis of an influence is not certain. Yet few authors on this matter have been able to avoid either a flat denial, on principle, or an enthusiastic acceptance, without criticism, of an influence from Andalusian Islam. Now it seems that one is reduced, in the current state of our knowledge, to a more sober attitude: the suspension of judgment while waiting for a truly conclusive document.[49]

In the second place, it is just as vain to imagine, continuing the image of the spring, that a large river would be something if the water coming from all of its tributaries did not flow into it. The history of culture is a continuity. Thus, as we have seen, the Greeks recognized that they were the heirs of

---

48　*Playground* is *cour de récréation* in French, and could be literally translated as a "court of recreation." [*translator's note.*]

49　As models of prudent and dispassionate debate, cf. J.-C. Vadet, *L'esprit courtois en Orient dans les cinq premiers siècles de l'Hégire* (Paris: Maisonneuve et Larose, 1968), p. 11 ff. and H.-I. Marrou, *Les troubadours* (Paris: Seuil, 1971), pp. 113–25.

the barbarians, and the Romans had a most vivid, and even a most painful consciousness of being latecomers in relation to the Greeks.[50]

It is necessary, then, to repair the injustice of the modern Occident toward the Arabic world by reviving the memory of such borrowings. But one must keep oneself, symmetrically, from inflicting the same injustice on the civilizations that preceded Islam by neglecting what Islam itself received from Hellenism, from Persia, or from the East Indies. For example, it is scientifically quite exact and politically very healthy to recall that Latin scholasticism received from "Arabism" not only a large part of its content, but even the formulation of the fundamental question of faith and reason.[51] And thought in Arabic language, in its two rival branches, itself inherited much from Hellenism. On the one hand, Arabic Aristotelianism (*falsafa*) claimed with Al-Farabi a continuous uninterrupted tradition: according to them, the *translatio studiorum* had been without a break from Alexandria to Baghdad.[52] On the other hand, the apologetic "theology" (*kalâm*) descended from a first attempt, already "scholastic" before its time, to reconcile Aristotelianism with Christian dogma. It was undertaken in Alexandria in the sixth century by John Philoponus, and continued, to cite only one name, by John of Damascus in the eighth century in the capital of the

---

50 Cf. *supra*, ch. II, p. 35 and 40.

51 This is the thesis developed by A. de Libera, *op. cit.*, ch. IV, "L'héritage oublié," pp. 98–142. I have borrowed from him his use of the term "Arabism," equally present in Renan.

52 Cf. M. Meyerhof, "Von Alexandrien nach Bagdad. Ein Beitrag zur Geschichte des philosophischen und medizinischen Unterrichts bei den Arabern," *Sitzungsberichte der Preussischen Akademie der Wissenschaften* (Philologisch-historische Klasse, 1930), pp. 389–429 and M. Mahdi, "Alfarabi against Philoponus," *Journal of Near Eastern Studies* XXVI, 4 (1967), pp. 233–60, especially 233–36. See the nuances in G. Strohmaier, "'Von Alexandrien nach Bagdad' – Eine fiktive Schultradition," *Aristoteles, Werk und Wirkung,* Paul Moraux gewidmet (Berlin and New York: De Gruyter, 1987), vol. II, pp. 380–89.

Omayyad Empire. The Middle Ages were entirely conscious of this.[53]

Let us keep ourselves, therefore, from isolating one or another moment from the permanent come and go that constitutes the history of Mediterranean culture, and that crystallizes sometimes in certain objects or certain words. One knows that a not insignificant part of Spanish vocabulary and that a significant quantity of scientific terms present in Occidental languages come from Arabic or through it as intermediary.[54] But there are words that have made a round trip or two. Thus, one knows that "apricot" comes from the Spanish *albaricoque*, itself derived (with a slight change of meaning) from the Arabic *al-barqûq*, "plum." But the Arabic derived from the Greek *praikokion*, from the Latin *praecocia*, "early ripened" (where we recognize our word "precocious"). Inversely, the modern Arabic *shik* is a calque from the French "chèque," with the same meaning. But the French word itself came from the Arabic *sakk*, "promissory note." And the academies of Arabic language wanted to banish the word "amalgame" before realizing that the French only returned to Arabic what they had previously borrowed. Words and the realities they designate have gone the complete cycle, and returned to the point of departure enriched by the evolution of a technique.

Never is one people an absolute origin. From the beginning everyone has been engaged in a mutual circulation and exchange. In their famous "Epistle of the Animals," the "Sincere Brethren" of Basra, at the beginning of the eleventh century, depicted the varying nations and religious communities in different scenes, each flattering themselves for their contributions to the treasure of human knowledge and reflec-

---

53   Cf. Maimonides, *Guide of the Perplexed*, I. 71; Joël, p. 122; English translation, Pines, p. 177 f.

54   Cf. the rich repertoire of G. B. Pellegrini, "L'elemento arabo nelle lingue neolatine con particolare riguardo all'Italia" in *L'Occidente e l'islam nell'alto medioevo* (Spoleto, 1965), pp. 697–790.

tion. Greece prided itself on the sciences developed by its people. The objection was then made that these sciences came from elsewhere, whether from Israel or Egypt. The Greek had no trouble recognizing this, and generalized:

> The wise man is right in what he says and, if it is true that we have borrowed from them, it's because our sciences as well as the sciences of other nations come from one another.[55]

The true problem is not located at the beginning, if that exists, but at the conclusion. It arises not so much in the somewhat vain search for the sources, as from reading history against the grain, undertaken as a search for one's ancestors by someone who believes himself a descendant. Research on the possible Arabic origin of certain traits of European civilization is overdetermined by the demands for originality in the reverse sense, on the part of the receivers as well as on that of their sources. Thus, when we try to see inventiveness as a privilege of the Greeks, we don't do that for the sake of the Greeks, but because we feel, or we imagine, more or less consciously, that the Greeks are, at bottom, ourselves.

The thesis of the present essay is exactly the opposite of any boastful claim to have invented everything in contrast to people who "invented nothing." To say that we are Romans is entirely the contrary of identifying ourselves with a prestigious ancestor. It is rather a divestiture, not a claim. It is to recognize that fundamentally we have invented nothing, but simply that we learned how to transmit a current come from higher up, without interrupting it, and all the while placing ourselves back in it.

---

55   *Rasā'il Iḫwān aṣ-Ṣafā'*, II, 8 [22], ed. Bustani (Beirut, 1983), vol. 2, p. 288.

V

Appropriation of the Foreign

Culture represents what a world has that is proper to it. It is what permits one to call this world, in another sense of the word, a "culture." Now what is proper is not necessarily present in the same way. I assert therefore that Europe distinguishes itself from other cultural worlds by its particular mode of relation to its own: the appropriation of what is perceived as foreign. This became a conscious fact for some. It was the case with Roger Bacon, the famous Franciscan of the thirteenth century. In the letter to Pope Clement IV that accompanied his works (1265), he pleaded among other things for the establishment of schools of languages in the Christian world. He argued thus:

> . . . the wisdom of the Latins is drawn from foreign languages; indeed, the entire sacred text and all philosophy have come down to us in external languages [sapientia latinorum tracta est ex alienis linguis; nam totus textus sacer et tota philosophia descenderunt a linguis extraneis][1]

I will translate the "wisdom of the Latins" in modern terms as "European culture." This culture is not Latin, or European, but foreign. Bacon, who took the trouble to learn some Greek and Hebrew, knew very well what his allusions

---

1   R. Bacon, *Lettera a Clemente IV,* ed. P. E. Bettoni, o.f.m. (Milan: 1964), p. 190.

referred to: the Bible is not in Latin, but in Hebrew and in Greek; "philosophy" – which during that period included nearly the entirety of profane culture – was for him deposited before all else in Greek works – Aristotle – and in Arabic works whose translations, in the twelfth and thirteenth centuries, had just renewed European learning. It is remarkable that Bacon should have expressed both the exteriority of the sources of European culture and the fact that they are, irreducibly, two.

One can support and deepen this intuition with a comparison between the way in which Europe on the one hand and on the other hand the Muslim and to a lesser extent the Byzantine cultural worlds conceived and practiced their relationship to the cultural heritage that preceded them.

Different Ways of Appropriating

The comparison of the processes of assimilation set in motion by the Latin world and the Arab world reveals a capital difference. It was already implicit in what I said above on the genre of works that the Arab world translated or didn't translate.[2] Very roughly, in the works that they translated, the Arabs concerned themselves with the content alone, while the Romans were in addition concerned with their literary aspect. The Arabs sought to appropriate a scientific and/or philosophical content that could constitute the truth. The Romans were also moved by aesthetic criteria. This was why the formal beauty of poetry could let through contents that conformed little to the reigning philosophical and moral orthodoxy. Thus, the atheist Lucretius was recopied by Christians; Ovid's *Art of Love* was recopied by people who had made

---

2   Cf., *supra*, ch. IV, p. 78. An interesting comparison between the Romans and the Arabs is sketched in W. von Humboldt, *Über die Verschiedenheit des menschlichen Sprachbaues und ihren Einfluß auf die geistige Entwicklung des Menschengeschlechts* (work on the Kawi), §34 in *Werke*, ed. A. Flitner and K. Giel, vol. 3 (Darmstadt: Wissenschaftliche Buchgesellschaft, 1963), p. 604.

vows of chastity, that is, the monks, and not necessarily Church Sunday monks, who nonetheless faithfully transcribed passages where the poet recommends synchronous orgasms . . .[3] Why? Because it was Lucretius, because it was Ovid. Ancient poetry, on the other hand, did not reach the Arab world. Or, if it was found there, it was in the form of anthologies of moral sententiae that became quite prosaic. This was the case because, as everyone knows, poetry is untranslatable. An Arabic author of the eleventh century, Al-Sijistâni, saw this clearly.[4] It was necessary, therefore, either not to read poetry at all, or to read it in the original, and consequentially, to preserve it in its original language.

Here, it seems to me, appears a decisive difference between the Arabic and the European transmission of ancient heritage. It is situated without doubt, first of all, on the linguistic level. The fundamental phenomenon was that of the presence or absence of a continuity of language. Latin and Greek survived in Christianity, which expressed itself by their means. In Islamized regions, on the contrary, Arabic caused Greek to disappear and progressively relegated Syriac and Coptic to the rank of purely liturgical languages or regional dialects. Persian would no doubt have suffered the same fate if it were not for the political and cultural renaissance begun in the eleventh century. As to Turkish and the languages of the countries Islamized later (India, Indonesia, and Africa), they entered the sphere of the Islamic world at a period after it had lost some of its original momentum.

There is an author who, even if he did not know a great deal about the Islamic religion, nonetheless saw the importance of this linguistic factor quite clearly: Machiavelli. He wrote about Christianity, for which he had little sympathy:

---

3   I remember an amusing remark on this subject by E. Gilson, but I have not succeeded in finding the reference.

4   Abu Sulayman al-Sijistânî, *The Muntakhab Siwân al-hikmah* . . . (in Arabic), intro. and notes by D. M. Dunlop (The Hague: Mouton, 1979), §96, p. 68.

It is true that they did not succeed in eliminating entirely the knowledge of the things done by its excellent men
[of the pagan civilization]. This arose from having maintained the Latin language, which they were forced to do
since they had to write this new law with it. For if they
had been able to write with a new language . . . we
would have not have any record of things past.[5]

If, in Europe, the new religion expressed itself in the vulgar language of the period, and afterward in the languages –
Germanic, Slavic, Celtic, etc. – of the newly converted peoples, it has not produced any particularly normative masterpiece of literature. One may judge the New Testament however one likes. One can underline the historical importance of
the story of the Passion – the highest majesty in the midst of
the most ignoble degradation – in crossing the barrier that
separated, until then, the elevated style from the low one.[6]
But it must be noted that the texts making it up are, as literary texts, of a somewhat mediocre quality. The Christians
have always known it and spoke, in allusion to the original
trade of the apostles, of a "language of fishermen" (*sermo
piscatorius*) or of a "humble speech."[7] And the same phenomenon can be observed on the profane level: the barbarian,
pagan tribes did not possess sufficiently elaborate languages
and a sufficiently rich literature to compete with those of the
territories on which they settled. In consequence, Europe had
to wait several centuries before literature appeared in the vulgar languages.

---

5 Machiavelli, *Discorsi sopra la prima deca di Tito Livio*, II, 5, in *Tutte le
   opere*, ed. Flora and Cordié, 2nd ed. (Mondadori, 1968), vol. 2, p. 247;
   English by H. C. Mansfield and N. Tarcov (Chicago and London: The
   University of Chicago Press, 1996), p. 139.

6 Cf. E. Auerbach, *Mimesis: The Representation of Reality in Western
   Literature*, tr. W. R. Trask (Princeton: Princeton University Press, 1953),
   ch. 2.

7 Cf. idem., "Sacrae scripturae sermo humilis" (in French) in *Gesammelte
   Aufsätze zur romanischen Philologie* (Berne/Munich: Francke, 1967), pp.
   21–26.

On the other hand, the Arabs possessed, before the Koran, great lyric, warlike, polemical poetry. They had besides and especially, since the adoption of Islam, an awareness of possessing in the Koran the unsurpassable literary masterpiece – even unequalable, as this inimitability constituted the great miracle, actually, the only miracle, supposed to attest to the divine origin of the sacred book.[8] Yet the Koranic revelation in no way interrupted or even deeply modified the Arabic poetic tradition: the same literary genres, and even the same themes, though not always very orthodox, flourished before as afterwards. The Koranic fact has exercised at most an indirect influence on Arabic literature. Indeed, one has been able to attribute to it the absence of an artistic prose in the land of the Islam, and the division of writing, on the one hand, into a poetry that alone rises to the level of art, and on the other, a prose of factual description. For once the Koran was supposed inimitable, it was dangerous to get too close to the rhythmical prose in which it was expressed.[9] Whatever the case may be, there was, then, outside of linguistic discontinuity, a second reason why the Arabs have not sought to adopt Greco-Latin poetry, and that is, quite simply, that they had no need to look elsewhere for what their own tradition provided in abundance.

The Best of Languages?

The two facts, religious and literary, combine into a single one, both resulting in a valorization – or not – of the language in which one expresses oneself. In Europe, this language is not considered as possessing a special value.[10] The Arabs, on the contrary, believe that they speak – or in any case that they read and write – the language of God himself. Indeed, the

---

8   Textual foundation in the Koran, XVII, 90; X, 39. Cf. *Encyclopaedia of Islam*, "I'DJĀZ," vol. III (1971), pp. 1018a–1020b (G. E. Grunebaum).

9   Cf. A. Miquel, *L'Orient d'une vie* (Paris: Payot, 1990), pp. 109 and 120.

10 Cf. *supra*, ch. II, p. 35f.

Koran has been revealed "in clear Arabic," and presents itself as "an Arabic Koran."[11] This religious origin is the basis of the valorization of the Arabic language; the poetry that came after the Koran is even supposed to be written in a language that is more beautiful than the poetry written before it.[12] In this way, Arabic, if it is not necessarily the most ancient language, would be the definitive language,[13] and in any case the clearest, the most concise, and the truest of languages.[14] Once a work is translated into Arabic, however, it acquires an incomparable dignity. It is elevated rather than adulterated. The copy, far from "degenerating from the vivacity of the original," is, one might say, elevated to a superior level. This is what was said by Al-Biruni, himself a native of Khwarezm, and so a speaker of Arabic as a second language:

> The sciences of every region of the world have been translated into the language of the Arabs, are embellished by it, have penetrated the hearts, and the beauty of the language has circulated in the veins and the arteries.[15]

11 Koran, XII, 2 and *passim*.

12 Cf. Ibn Khaldûn, *Muqaddimah*, IV; Q, vol. 2, p. 269 ff.; R, vol. 2, p. 303 ff. and VI; Q, vol. 3, p. 350, 1–8; R, vol. 3, p. 396 ff.

13 Cf. A. Borst, *Der Turmbau von Babel. Geschichte der Meinungen über Ursprung und Vielfalt der Sprachen und Völker* (Stuttgart: A. Hiersemann, 1957), vol. 1: *Fundamente und Aufbau*, p. 334.

14 Cf. for example, *Rasā' il Ikhwān aṣ-Ṣafā'*, III, 9 (40), ed. Bustani (Beirut: 1983), vol. 3, p. 377 and 381, or Ibn Khaldûn, *Muqaddimah*, VI; Q, vol. 3, p. 280, 1; R, vol. 3, p. 321; and Q, vol. 3, p. 300, 1 ff; R, vol. 3, p. 344. Cf. also aš-Sāfi'ī, *ar-Risāla*, §138, Säkir, p. 42, ed. A. M. cited in J. Langhade, *Du Coran à la philosophie. La langue arabe et la formation du vocabulaire philosophique de Farabi* (Damas, 1994), p. 117.

15 Preface to the *Book of Drugs* in Al-Biruni's *Book on Pharmacy and Materia Medica*, ed. and trans. into English by Hakim Mohammed Said (Karachi: Hamdard National Foundation, 1973), p. 12, 3 ff.; English translation, pp. 7b–8a. Cf. also Abū Ḥātim ar-Rāzī, *Kitāb az-Zīna fi 'l-kalimāt al-'arabiyya*, ed. Al-Ḥamdānī vol. I, p. 63, 2–4, cited in J. Langhade, *op. cit.*, p. 148.

It is not surprising, then, that the original versions of translated works have been neglected. Accordingly, one only occasionally meets an interest among the Muslims in Greek language and the culture of the Greeks, and most of the time it is only where Arabic doesn't dominate exclusively. This is the case with the Turks, for example, during the reign of Mehmed the Conqueror.[16]

One finds analogous cases at Byzantium, but for different reasons. Byzantium shared with Europe a linguistic continuity between the period that preceded and the period that followed the arrival of the dominant religion. It is what distinguished both of them from the Arab world. This continuity was, of course, the Greek language. But, on the other hand, Byzantium had a characteristic in common with the Arab world that distinguished it from Europe. For Byzantium was itself also conscious of the presence of a valorized language, one illustrated by the masterpieces of a prestigious literature – the Greek of Homer and Plato. Thus, Theodorus Metochites, in the fourteenth century, could proudly exclaim:

> The states neighboring on Hellas have not had a share in a similar tradition. Indeed, they do not possess a language triumphantly established for all time that, by its aesthetic charm, has attracted the majority of men into its world.[17]

The classical form of this language remained normative, so much so that one sometimes sought to elevate the dignity of certain texts by a paradoxical translation that made them de-evolve linguistically, from popular Greek to learned Greek. Thus, in the tenth century, Simeon Metaphrastes rewrote in

---

16 For clarification, cf. J. Raby, "Mehmet the Conqueror's Greek Scriptorium," *Dumbarton Oaks Papers* 37 (1983), pp. 15–34.

17 *Ethikos è peri paideias*, f. 205r, cited in H. Hunger, "Theodoros Metochites als Vorläufer des Humanismus in Byzanz," *Byzantinische Zeitschrift* 45 (1952), pp. 4–19, cited in a note to p. 15.

cultivated Greek all the lives of the saints which popular piety had written in its language.[18] The linguistic continuity maintained by learned Greek has maintained (though at the price of a scholarly apprenticeship) the accessibility of the ancient masterpieces. This was obtained through a fiction, that of the unity of the Greek language. And it may be that the continuity of Hellenism, from Homer (lest we go back to Linear B) to the Byzantines, is itself only a fiction.[19] As to the language, in any event, the real separation between a "purified" (*katharevousa*) and a popular (*dhimotiki*) language would not cease to increase until its latest consequences, politically overdetermined, in contemporary Greece.[20] And in any event, the cultural elites of Byzantium never felt alienated in regard to ancient Greece.

Thus, unlike Byzantium, Europe has not been able to perdure through the continuity of a language that had been the support of a very great literature, in peaceable possession of a classical heritage that assured it the feeling of cultural superiority. Nor, like the Muslim world, has it been able to compensate for its initial dependence on exterior sources through the impression of ennobling and enlarging the knowledge it inherited in making it attain the language chosen by God for His ultimately unadulterated message, and by diffusing it over the territory His definitive religion covered. Europe, therefore, had to confront a consciousness of having borrowed, without hope of restitution, from a source that it could neither regain nor surpass.

---

18 Cf. *Dictionnaire de spiritualité*, "Syméon Métaphraste," col. 1383–86 (M.-H. Congourdeau).

19 Cf. C. Mango, "Byzantinism and Romantic Hellenism," *Journal of the Warburg and Courtauld Institutes* XXVIII (1965), pp. 29–43. For the opposing view, cf. Ap. Vacalopoulos, "Byzantinism and Hellenism. Remarks on the Racial Origin and the Intellectual Continuity of the Greek Nation" in *Balkan Studies* IX (1968), pp. 101–26.

20 Cf. R. Fontaine, "L'Eglise grecque et la question de la langue en Grèce," *Istina* 21 (1976), pp. 412–29.

Dwarfed and Nostalgic

European culture is in this way marked by the melancholic feeling of an alienation or inferiority in relation to a source, which provokes a sense of nostalgia. One can find traces of this sentiment at different periods. Thus, in the Middle Ages, one sees the recurrent image according to which a later period perceives itself as a generation of dwarfs that need to perch on the shoulders of the giants that preceded them. This image is found probably for the first time at the beginning of the twelfth century in Bernard of Chartres (who died around 1125), for whom the giant was Aristotle.[21] It is next met among Christians from the same epoch,[22] but also among Jews for whom it permitted the illustration of the juridical principle according to which the *halakhah* is regulated by the decisions of the most recent interpreters.[23] It came to a climax, at the end of a turbulent history, with Newton.[24] But the comparison of the Ancients with the Giants and of the Moderns with the Dwarfs is also implicit in Swift who presents the former in his description of Brobdingnag and the latter in that of Lilliput. In addition, it is remarkable to note that the same image permitted the encapsulation of two different relations to the past, the profane as well as the religious: scenes of stained glass at Chartres represent the four Evangelists perched on the shoulders of the prophets of the old Covenant.

The same feeling is present at the start of modern times, for example in Montaigne, who wrote:

---

21 Cited by John of Salisbury, *Metalogicon* III, 4; *Patrologiae Cursus, Series Latina* 199, 900c.

22 Cf. E. Jeauneau, "'Nani gigantum humeris insidentes.' Essai d'interprétation de Bernard de Chartres," *Vivarium* 5 (1967), pp. 79–99.

23 Cf. D. Zlotnik, "On the source of the simile 'dwarf and giant' and its avatars" (in Hebrew), *Sinai* 77 (1975), pp. 184–189.

24 Cf the both erudite and amusing book by Robert K. Merton, *On the Shoulders of Giants. A Shandean Postscript* (New York: Free Press, 1965), 290 pp.

> The productions of these great rich minds of the past are
> very far beyond the utmost stretch of my imagination
> and desire. Their writings not only satisfy and fill me,
> but astound me and transfix me with admiration. I judge
> their beauty; I see it, if not to the utmost, at least enough
> so that I cannot aquire to it myself.[25]

This feeling sometimes feeds on a general conception of history as decadence in relation to a primitive truth. But it cannot be reduced to that. Even after the seventeenth century
and the quarrel of the Ancients and the Moderns which saw,
however, the victory of the latter, and even after the eighteenth century and the accession of the idea of progress to the
rank of an unassailable belief, it survived in an underground
fashion in German romanticism and idealism.[26] One finds it
still in Goethe who wrote:

> To maintain ourselves courageously at the height of
> these barbarian advantages, since no doubt we can never
> attain the level of the ancient advantages, such is our
> duty.[27]

Finally, Nietzsche formulated it in regard to the whole of
German philosophy:

> German philosophy taken as a whole . . . is the gravest
> kind of *romanticism* and nostalgia that has ever existed: a

---

25 Montaigne, *Essais*, II, 17, "De la présomption," ed. P. Villey (Alcan,
    1930), vol. 2, p. 610. English tr. D. M. Frame (Stanford, Ca: Stanford
    University Press, 1958), p. 482 f. I owe this reference as well as the pas-
    sage from Goethe that follows to the article of P. Meitinger, "De
    l'Europe considérée en sa littérature," *Cahiers de l'Ecole des sciences
    philosophiques et religieuses*, Facultés universitaires Saint-Louis,
    Bruxelles, 14 (1993), pp. 49–94, cited on p. 51.

26 Cf. J. Taminiaux, *La nostalgie de la Grèce à l'aube de l'idéalisme allemand.
    Kant et les Grecs dans l'itinéraire de Schiller, de Hölderlin et de Hegel* (La
    Haye: Nijhoff, 1967), 274 pp.

27 Goethe, "Notes sur 'Le neveu de Rameau'" in *Sämtliche Werke . . .*
    Münchner Ausgabe, vol. 7 (Munich: Hanser, 1991), p. 666.

demand for the very best that ever existed. Since then, one is not at all at home – one demands, at bottom, to return to where one can feel at home in one way or another, because it is there alone that one would like to be at home, and that is – in the Greek world! Only all the bridges leading there are collapsed – with the exception of the rainbows of concepts! And they lead everywhere, toward all the hometowns and "fatherlands" that have ever been given to Greek souls![28]

And Leo Strauss, in our century, still recognized that "one must be swayed by a sincere longing for the past."[29]

Between Historicism and Aestheticism

It is this feeling, I would suggest, that makes "Romans" out of Europeans. And in a sense, we have remained Romans even after and despite the revolution that has taken place in our relationship to the past. One must begin by becoming aware of the extent of that revolution. It is silent, but nonetheless constitutes one of the fundamental traits of modernity, it is the revolution in our historical relationship to our past. No doubt no one saw this better than Nietzsche, in the second of the *Untimely Meditations* (1874),[30] which remains the indispensable starting point for all reflection on this subject. The historicization of the past is the fact that one preserves the past, not because it is beautiful, or pertinent, or as one would want to say – which would be to return to considering it as present – but rather for the singular reason that it is past and therefore "interesting." One can point out several signs of this fact. Witness the fantastic, even malignant production of his-

28 Nietzsche, fragment of August-September 1885, 41 [4] *Kritische Studienausgabe*, vol. 11, p. 678.

29 Leo Strauss, "On Collingwood's Philosophy of History," *Review of Metaphysics* 5 (1951–52), p. 576.

30 Nietzsche, "On the Advantage and Disadvantage of the Study of History for Life." Cf also my own sketch, "Culture et mémoire," *Grand Larousse annuel*, Le livre de l'année, 1994, pp. 29–31.

torical works. Or again, consider the phenomenon of the museum,[31] more visible still when no longer satisfied with preserving the major works of art whose beauty tears them from their dated context and confers on them some atemporal value, but goes toward a progressive museumization of all the past.[32] Or again, witness the monument to the dead, supposed to memorialize the "war to end all wars," and therefore of what never again ought to be real. Our relationship to the Ancients has become a relationship of conservation: we edit or study ancient texts, even when their content has nothing more to do with our knowledge or beliefs.

This attitude toward the ancient texts is tied to another that compensates for it and is perhaps its antidote: the aesthetic attitude that makes one appreciate a text for its beauty. This is what explains this paradoxical gesture of appropriating what one feels has nevertheless become strange. Now what characterizes the aesthetic attitude before a reality is that the separation of form and content loses all its pertinence. It suffices to have read a poem or a novel once in one's life to know it. The impossibility of distinguishing the content quite obviously permits the protection of the form. But it is also necessary to understand that this impossibility protects the content just as well. Changing the form to keep the content (which happens in a translation) reduces the text to the understanding of the translator. At the same time, it prevents other interpreters from coming along and digging out the meaning. The work of hermeneutics is possible only if the letter is preserved. And therefore if one has read the entire text, even the most prosaic, like a poem in which each word is itself irreplaceable – or, in a sense, if one reads prose as a limited case of poetry. The advantage of an aesthetic relationship to the texts is thus that it postulates that the text is inex-

---

31 The essential reading on this is without doubt in Valéry, "Le problème des musées," *Œuvres*, Bibliothèque de la Pléiade, vol. 2, pp. 1290–93.

32 Cf. H. Lübbe, *Zeit-Verhältnisse. Zur Kulturphilosophie des Fortschritts*, Styria, Graz *et al.*, 1983, pp. 9–32.

haustible. It is its "inexhaustibility," and not its value as a model, that gives a text the character of a "classic." As Schlegel says:

> It is not necessary that one understand a classical text completely. But those who are cultivated and who cultivate themselves must always want to draw more lessons from it.[33]

A classic text is a text from which one can always extract new ideas. Now what one might call the cultural bet of Europe is just that these ancient texts will always have something to teach us – and therefore, that they must be preserved in their literalness.

Throwing Away the Shell

The world of Islam, on the other hand, if it has translated, and it has translated extensively, and if it has prolonged the content of what it translates, has not preserved the originals. Once again it is Friedrich Schlegel who noticed it, in a passage of polemical appearance, but whose central idea seems to me right:

> The Arabs are of an extremely polemical nature, the annihilators among the nations. The mania they had (*Liebhaberei*) of erasing the originals, or of throwing them out when the translation was finished, characterizes the spirit of their philosophy. It is no doubt because of this that they were infinitely more cultivated (*kultiviert*), but, despite all their civilization (*Kultur*), purely and simply more barbarian (*barbarisch*) than the Europeans of the Middle Ages. For the barbarian is indeed he who is at the same time anti-classical and anti-progressive.[34]

---

33 F. Schlegel, *Kritische Fragmente*, §20; *Kritische Ausgabe*, vol. 2, p. 149.

34 F. Schlegel, *"Athenäum"-fragmente*, §229; *Kritische Ausgabe*, vol. 2, p. 202. For mysterious reasons, I didn't remember this text, that I had nonetheless already read, at the time of the first edition of the present work. I don't know where Schlegel came by this information.

One can put the value judgment aside that, in this case, is unfavorable, but preserve the fact, which is attested elsewhere. It had besides already sparked a reflection of Ibn Khaldûn who said magnificently:

> (The Muslims) desired to learn the sciences of the (foreign) nations. They made them their own through translations. They pressed them into the mold of their own views. They peeled (*ǧarrada*) off these strange tongues (*luġa*) [and make them pass] into their [own] idiom (*lisān*), and surpassed the achievements of (the non-Arabs) in them. The manuscripts in the non-Arabic languages were forgotten, abandoned, and scattered. All the sciences came to exist in Arabic. The systematic works on them were written in (Arabic) writing. Thus, students of the sciences needed a knowledge of the meaning of (Arabic) words and (Arabic) writing. They could dispense with all other languages, because they had been wiped out and there was no longer any interest in them.[35]

One has to examine each image. One will notice in particular the image implicitly contained in the verb that I have translated very etymologically as "peel," and which commonly means "skin," and even, in philosophy, "abstract": that of a fruit whose pulp one consumes and whose skin one then throws away. In any event, the consequence of this disappearance of the original texts and of the neglect of the original languages is that the Muslim world has not been able to return to what it translated and deepen their examination. Admittedly, there are examples of a retranslation of the same Greek text. But this all happened in the ninth and tenth centuries when, of course, the originals were still available. This was as true of the Muslims as, in their wake, for the Christians of Syriac culture. It has been pointed out that these latter, in the ninth century, began to reuse some Greek manuscripts

---

35 Cf. Ibn Khaldûn, *Muqaddimah*, VI; Q, vol. 3, p. 276, 11–19; English trans. R, vol. 3, p. 317 – modified.

whose surface they scraped in order to write on them, not out of any lack of interest in Hellenic heritage, but because the works were already available in translation.[36]

In doing this, the Islamized world made the phenomena of "renaissances" impossible – that is, of a return to the original texts against the traditions that claimed to follow them. In the European world, the presence of the originals made a constant process of appeal possible. The schools of thought could confront each other with more or less bitterness. But at least they argued around the same sources. The "renaissances" are nothing other than the challenging of an ancient reading by a new reading of the same body of texts. Thus, the Italians, for example at Padua, opposed to the Scholastic's Aristotle that of Averroes, which was supposed, and not without reason, to be closer to the historical Aristotle. Or again, the humanists played the Latin of Cicero off the supposedly "barbaric" Medieval Latin.

Inclusion and Digestion

The same example of the reception of Aristotle can help to characterize the Islamic style of reception of ancient heritage and to better perceive, in contrast, that which characterizes Europe. One can indeed distinguish two types of reception. I propose to call them inclusion and digestion. As a child, I was fascinated by the knick-knacks on sale along the coast or in the mountains in which one drowned in translucent plastic, according to the case, a sea horse or an edelweiss. This is called "inclusion." The mass that surrounds the object removes it from one's immediate grasp. On the other hand, it also maintains it in a certain position, chosen because it permits one to see it as best possible. And already it shelters it

---

36   Cf. S. Brock, "From Antagonism to Assimilation: Syriac Attitudes to Greek Learning," N. Garsoian *et al.* (eds,), *East of Byzantium. Syria and Armenia in the Formative Period*, Dumbarton Oaks Symposium, 1980 (Washington: Dumbarton Oaks Papers, 1982), p. 29.

from the surrounding air whose contact would cause it to decompose. In this model, the interior does not stop for all that being something other. It is rather just the fact of having become interior that maintains it in its otherness. I will therefore call *inclusion*[37] that appropriation in which the foreign body is maintained in its otherness and surrounded by the process of an appropriation whose very presence brings out its otherness. On the other hand, I will call *digestion* an appropriation in which the object is assimilated to such a point that it loses its independence. This suppresses the difference between the subject who appropriates and the object that he appropriates: the lion is made from the digested lamb.

Inclusion is a highly artificial procedure; digestion is the most elementary of natural processes. If, therefore, the relationship of Europe to its sources is, as we will have to see, not natural but artificial, it would not be surprising to discover that Europe distinguishes itself from the other daughters of the ancient world less by the content it appropriated than by the way in which it appropriated it. Nor is there anything surprising in the fact that this way is artificial rather than natural. Ancient art and literature were included, as such, by inclusion as *others* in the transparency of European culture.

Let's give some specific examples. Where what must be received is a written text, two literary genres correspond to each of these two types of reception. First, the commentary reproduces the text, lemma after lemma, and explores it while maintaining its otherness. Secondly, the text can be integrated through rewriting into a work from which the original text can no longer be distinguished – what one calls a paraphrase. If then one considers the different ways Aristotle was commented on, in localizing them by culture and setting them back in their time, one notices the following facts: the ancient Greek commentators practiced the commentary as well as the

---

37 I am generalizing a concept (*Einsetzung*) borrowed from K. Flasch, *Einführung in die Philosophie des Mittelalters* (Darmstadt: Wissenschaftliche Buchgesellschaft, 1989), p. 2.

paraphrase, as Themistius (fourth century of our era) did. But
the great Neo-Platonic commentators, like Simplicius (sixth
century) preferred the commentary. We possess commentaries from Al-Farabi (tenth century), for example, on the
Treatise on Interpretation, as well as shorter texts that rework
certain treatises of the *Organon* by adapting their content,
though under the same title.

Avicenna (eleventh century) represents a decisive turn.
He systematically practiced the method of the paraphrase, a
method of inclusion, notably by rewriting the whole of the
Aristotelian system of the sciences in his vast encyclopedia,
The Healing (*Kitāb aš-sifā'*). It is of little importance to point out
here the evidence that, first, he added an elevated dose of
Neo-Platonism, which at that time followed Aristotelianism
like a shadow, and secondly, that he created, in giving the
work the stamp of his own genius, something profoundly
original. What is important to note here is that Avicenna perfectly represents the Islamic method of appropriation by
incorporation. One can recognize some affinity between the
styles of appropriation and the religious background:
Avicenna was, first, consciously opposed to the Arab
Christians, the Aristotelizers of Baghdad. And secondly, looking back, he is distinguished for us from an author who, like
Averroes, could hardly be received except by the Jews and the
Christians. Now, the enterprise of Avicenna succeeded completely. So well that, in the Muslim Orient, Aristotelianism
quite simply became Avicennism.[38] The receiver absorbed
what he received to the point of being confounded with him,
and of making him inaccessible for a direct reception.

Averroes (twelfth century), in a sort of return to the
method of Al-Farabi, proceeded in two ways, depending on
the genre of the commentary he was writing. He proceeded
by digestion in his epitomes (*ğawāmi'*) and his so-called "middle" commentaries (*šarḥ*), and by inclusion in his "great"

38 Cf. D. Gutas, *Avicenna and the Aristotelian Tradition. Introduction to
Reading Avicenna's Philosophical Works* (Leiden: Brill, 1988), p. 261.

commentaries (*tafsīr*). Among the Christians, unlike his master Albert the Great, who proceeded like Avicenna, Thomas Aquinas (thirteenth century) wrote only great commentaries that all went back to the method of the commentaries of Averroes. With regard to the exegetic works of Averroes, one observes a very interesting inversion between the Jewish and the Christian philosophers. The passage of the Jewish intellectual centers from the Muslim world to the Christian accompanied an evolution in the styles of appropriation: in the beginning, the Jews used epitomes and not the great commentaries; on the other hand, the Christians used the great commentaries right away, and hardly knew the epitomes before the Renaissance. It was only in the wake of Christian scholasticism that the Jews came to be interested in the great commentaries of Averroes, and therefore, in the text itself of Aristotle.[39]

Why this model of relationship to cultural borrowings? As to the written texts, one can think that the presence and the linguistic accessibility of great poetry had imposed on Europe the aesthetic model of relationship to the text. As a result, it prevented one from decanting the content of the work all at once in order to throw away the container. In this sense it was poetry that saved Europe. But it would not have been able to do it if Christianity had not already, on the level of the relationship to the Absolute, imposed the cultural model of secondarity.

---

39 Cf. Zonta, *op. cit.*, p. 151 and *passim*.

VI

An Eccentric Identity

Indeed, as we have seen,[1] in the Christian world, the phenomenon of secondarity is found up to and including the relationship with the Absolute (to put it clearly, religion). Now it seems to me that it is the presence of secondarity on this fundamental level that singularizes Europe. Indeed, even if other civilizations recognize themselves as heirs – as many Asian cultures recognize a heavy debt to India (Southeast Asia, Tibet) or to China (Japan, Korea) – Europe is perhaps the only one to make this secondarity a principle situated at the very center of its relationship to the Absolute.

The Religious Basis of Secondarity

The elevation of cultural secondarity to the level of the relationship with the Absolute is the accomplishment of the religion that decisively marked Europe, that is to say, Christianity. It knew itself to be second in relation to the Old Covenant. This anchorage in the Absolute gave this secondarity a unique weight, though not without modifying it. Indeed, secondarity, in the religious domain, is not a question of time: the Old Covenant is not a past from which the New one distanced itself progressively; it is rather a permanent foundation. Consequentially, the New Covenant does not

---

1   Cf. *supra*, ch. III, p. 64.

conceive of itself as a progress in relation to the past, nor therefore as a historicization of the past. Conversely, the relationship to the heritage of the ancient world is indeed a relation to a past, and as such, it cannot avoid these two phenomena. Cultural secondarity (toward the "Greek"), then, must be retaken in the religious secondarity (toward the "Jewish") in order to be able to provide a permanent model.

In this way, it was religious secondarity that prevented all culture inherited from Christianity, as is the case with Europe, from considering itself as its own source. The refusal of Marcionism[2] is thus, perhaps, the founding event of the history of Europe as a civilization, in that it furnished the matrix of the European relationship to the past and anchored it at the highest possible level. It may be then that Saint Irenaeus, from his polemics against Marcionism and his affirmation of the identity of the God of the Old Testament with that of the New, is not only one of the Fathers of the Church, but also one of the Fathers of Europe. Conversely, the withdrawal of Europe into its own culture, understood as being only one culture among others, would be something like cultural Marcionism. In the religious domain as in the cultural domain, Europe had the same relation to what preceded it: it did not tear itself from the past, nor did it reject it. Europe did not pretend, as to profane culture, to have absorbed in itself everything that Hellenism contained or, in religion, everything that the Old Testament contained – in such a way that one could throw away the empty shell. At the most, what Christianity claims to possess (the term is not even right) is the key permitting the interpretation of that to which the Old Covenant tended. It claims that the recapitulation of past history is given in the event of the Christ, the plenitude of the divinity (Colossians 2:9). But the exploration of the riches that are contained there, and their refraction in the sainthood of the Church, is an infinite task, which requires nothing less than all of history to come.

---

2   Cf. *supra*, ch. III, p. 57.

The Islamic religion, in contrast, is characterized by an attitude of absorption. For the Islamic religion, as we have seen,[3] the Jews and the Christians tampered with the texts of revelation that were transmitted to them. Such revelation is present in its purity only in the Koran. It follows, for the Islamic religion, that the truth of Judaism, as well as that of Christianity, is found within itself, and in it alone. This truth is situated therefore outside the two religions that have preceded it and that are thus alienated from themselves. In consequence, their study has no intrinsic interest. Now, everything happens in the Muslim world as if the same model had been applied to the anterior or external civilizations. Islamic civilization has admittedly been able to interest itself in them, and even describe them in sumptuous detail in its masterpieces of physical and human geography.[4] This is a trait that it shares with Europe,[5] and that, on the other hand, distinguishes it from Byzantium.[6] But Islamic civilization, in contrast to Europe, has hardly dreamed of using its knowledge of the foreign as an instrument that would permit it, through comparison and distancing in relation to itself, to understand itself by becoming conscious of the non-obvious character of its cultural practices.[7] It may be that its geographers made a eulogy of India and of China in order to address a discrete critique of the Islamic civilization of their time, often compensated in the last instance by an affirmation of the religious superiority of the latter.[8] The examples that one could find of

---

3   Cf. *ibid.*, p. 60.

4   On the Arab geographers, see the synthesis of A. Miquel, *La géographie humaine du monde musulman jusqu'au milieu du XIe siècle,* 4 vol. (Paris: Mouton, 1967, 1975, 1980, 1988).

5   Cf. *infra.* Ch. VII, p. 139.

6   Cf. C. Mango, *Byzantine Literature as a Distorting Mirror* (Oxford: Clarendon Press, 1975), p. 17.

7   This is the central thesis of B. Lewis, *The Muslim Discovery . . . , op. cit.* Cf. also Grunebaum, *Islam . . .* , pp. 43, 46, 47f.

8   Cf. Miquel, *Orient . . .* , note to p. 170.

such a vision "reflected" in the mirror are exceptional and come from marginal or heretical thinkers. Thus, the contact with the Brahmin Hindu thinkers whose religion does quite well without prophecy (which the Islamic religion declares on the contrary necessary to the happiness of man and to a good social order) posed a problem for the Muslim thinkers; the real or fictitious dialogue with the Brahmins was able to serve to mask a critique of the Islamic religion in a free thinker like Ibn al-Rawandi.[9]

The only incontestable exception is without doubt the astonishing work of Al-Biruni on India.[10] This universal scholar (973–1048), astronomer, geographer, historian, mineralogist, pharmacologist, etc.,[11] had taken the trouble to learn enough Sanskrit to be able to translate in both directions between this language and Arabic (for him also a learned language). He presented a tableau of Hindu society and beliefs with perfect impartiality. The sole predecessor whom he recognized, the mysterious Eranshahri, had according to him, been able to give an undistorted image of Christianity, Judaism, and Manichaeism because he himself was attached to no existing religion.[12] Admittedly, Biruni affirmed his orthodoxy, but the fact that he had taken the care to present, in one and the same work, the bibliography of his writings

9   Cf. P. Kraus, "Studien zur islamischen Ketzergeschichte. Das Kitāb az-Zumurrud des Ibn ar-Rawāndī" (1933–34), reprinted in *Alchemie, Ketzerei, Apokryphen im frühen Islam. Gesammelte Aufsätze* (Hildesheim: Olms, 1994), pp. 109–90; S. Stroumsa, "The Blinding Emerald: Ibn ar-Rawandī's Kitāb az-Zumurrud" *Journal of the American Oriental Society* 114–12 (1994), pp. 163–85.

10   Al-Birūnī *Tahgīg mā li-'l-Hind min magūla magbūla fī 'l-'agl aw mardūla*, ed. 'Ali Ṣafā (Beirut, 1983), 536 pp.; English trans. E. Sachau, *Alberuni's India* (London, Kegan Paul, 1914).

11   One can form an idea of his work thanks to the very good anthology of G. Strohmaier, *In den Gärten der Wissenschaft. Ausgewählte Texte aus den Werken des muslimischen Universalgelehrten* (Leipzig: Reclam, 1991), 318 pp.

12   *Taḥqīq . . .*, op. cit., p. 15, 12–17; Engl. Sachau, vol. I, p. 6.

and those of the free-thinker Râzî invites one to ask questions . . .[13] In any event, this grandiose exception unfortu-
nately does nothing but confirm the rule, since Al-Biruni
remained without intellectual posterity.

The Idea of a "Renaissance"

In the cultural history of Europe, what I have called cultural
secondarity seems to me to govern the relationship to the
other. This relationship can be summarized in a double movement, of diastole and systole. First, one observes a constant
expansion toward a supposedly "barbarian" domain that was
to be assimilated and integrated. One can understand, from
this point of view, at the very beginning of European history,
the integration of peoples whose language was not Latin;
first the Germanic tribes, then the Slavic or Scandinavian, and
their access to writing, and to Christianity. Or again, the
expansion that followed the great discoveries, and ended in
the colonial adventure and in the sharing between European
or quasi-European nations almost the totality of the inhabited
world.

Secondly, one witnesses a constant effort to go back up
toward the classical sources. One can thus describe the intellectual history of Europe as an almost uninterrupted train of
renaissances. I must first clarify this idea somewhat. It insert-
ed itself first of all in a determined schema of intellectual history, inherited from Petrarch,[14] then taken up again in the ideology of the Enlightenment. This ternary schema, which is
perhaps the result of a secularization of Joachim of Fiore, presupposed a brilliant period that would come to interrupt a
period of darkness, the "dark ages," the "ténèbres." This
period would come to a close, and it would be necessary to

---

13 *Epître de Berūni contenant le répertoire des ouvrages de Muḥammad b.
   Zakarīya ar-Rāzī,* ed. P. Kraus, *(Paris:* Matba'at al-Qalam, *1936), 51 pp.*

14 Cf. Th. E. Mommsen, "Petrarch's Conception of the 'Dark Ages,'"
   Speculum XVII (1942), pp. 226–42.

retrieve the initial clarity. In doing this, one spanned an empty age, supposedly empty, that was sufficiently defined by its intermediary position, the "Middle Ages." The Renaissance, therefore, became the name of the end of the medieval obscurity.

For their part, historians have shown that the phenomenon of a renaissance, as a return and recourse to the ancient, had in fact never ceased. They enlarged the concept of renaissance and described its continuity over the centuries. One can then begin with the "Carolingian Renaissance," proceed to the "Renaissance of the Twelfth Century,"[15] and continue, of course, with the series of Italian renaissances. But one could not stop there, because one finds the German cycle of Hellenism in the same line. One can make it begin with Winckelmann – unless one insists on going back to Beatus Rhenanus. Weimar classicism then followed and resulted in the dream of becoming Greeks once again. This project was first of all entertained by the Romanticism of Jena, as Schlegel put it:

> To live according to the classical fashion, and to realize Antiquity in oneself in a practical fashion – such was the summit and the goal of philology.[16]

Then it was taken up by Nietzsche in the continuation of the fragment we just cited:

> From day to day we become more Greek, first, as is well understood, in our concepts and our evaluations, as phantoms who play at being Greek; but one day, we may hope, also with our bodies! There resides (and has always resided) my hope for what is German![17]

---

15 An expression launched by C. H. Haskins, *The Renaissance of the Twelfth Century* (Cambridge: Harvard University Press, 1927).

16 F. Schlegel, *"Athenäum Fragmente,"*§147; KA, vol. 2, p. 188.

17 Nietzsche, fragment of August-September 1885, 41 [4]; KSA, vol. 11, p. 679, *Wille zur Macht*, §419 ff. Cf. *supra*, p. 101f.

The dream of a new renaissance is still present in the
thinkers of our century. Outside the somewhat foggy dreams
of a "third humanism" in Werner Jaeger, Heidegger had an
ambiguous attitude on this subject.[18] Leo Strauss himself
dreamed of a new renaissance founded on the idea of natural
right:

> At most he hoped there might someday be a third
> humanism, or renaissance, after those of Italy and
> Germany, but this time inspired neither by the visual
> beauty of the Greeks' statues, paintings, and buildings
> nor by the grandeur of their poetry, but by the truth of
> their philosophy.[19]

Muslim Humanism and European Humanism

Is this fact proper to Europe? What about the other cultural
domains? Can one speak, for example, of a Muslim humanism? The question is debated, and all the more as the word
itself is far from being univocal. Let us try to introduce a little
clarity on this subject:

a) One can understand "humanism" as the attempt to create a world founded solely on the consideration of man and
by setting God outside of that circuit. Thus, in modern
English, *humanist* is a polite expression for "atheist." In this
sense, it is clear that a Muslim humanism is contradictory, just
as much as would be a Christian humanism.

b) If one understands by "humanism" the love of belles-
lettres, one can find in the Arab world periods during which
the social conditions necessary to the emergence of such a

---

18   Cf. the references given in my essay, "La phénoménologie comme
     accès au monde grec . . ." in *Phénoménologie et métaphysique*, ed. J.-L.
     Marion and G. Planty-Bonjour (Paris: Presses Universitaires de France,
     1984), p. 249, nt. 9.

19   Allan Bloom, "Leo Strauss. September 20, 1899–October 18, 1973,"
     Giants and Dwarfs: Essay 1960–1990 (New York: Simon & Schuster,
     1990), p. 252.

humanism coincided: a public for refined letters, a taste for a general and particularly literary culture, etc., and where these conditions bore fruit entirely comparable to that in Europe. Some savvy experts have thus been able to propose calling certain characteristics of the Muslim world "humanist." This is the case, following I. Guidi and A. Badawi, of L. Gardet,[20] and then of M. Arkoun.[21]

c) One can call "humanism" the valorization of man, supposedly placed at the summit of nature or, for religions, of the creation. One finds in the Islamic world some affirmations of the exceptional value of man, beginning with the passages of the Koran on the role of man as the lieutenant (caliph) of God on earth.[22] One finds analogous affirmations in a good many anterior or parallel cultural traditions, in the Bible as among the Greeks.[23] In the lands of Islamic religion, one also finds a theory of the "perfect man," alone worthy of a supreme place among the living.[24] In this way, one may speak of a humanism in Arabic thought.

But first, if its tenets are expressed in Arabic, it comes from an oriental, Iranian or Greek, source.[25] And secondly, can one attach humanism to the Islamic religion as if it were

---

20 L. Gardet, *La cité musulmane* (Paris: Vrin, 1954), pp. 271–328.

21 Cf. M. Arkoun, *Contribution à l'étude de l'humanisme arabe au IVe-Xe siècle. Miskawayh philosophe et historien* (Paris: Vrin, 1970), especially the very nuanced remarks in "L'attitude humaniste," pp. 356–64.

22 Koran, II, 27–30. The text is not absolutely certain. Blachère, French trans., p. 736, suspects "creature" (*ḫalīqa*) in the place of "caliph" (*ḫalīfa*). But it has been traditionally interpreted in the sense I assume. Cf. Wadād al-Qāḍī, "The Term 'Khalifa' in Early Exegetic Literature," *Welt des Islams* 28 (1988), pp. 392–411.

23 Psalm 8; for the Greeks, cf. the references given in my *Aristote . . .* , *op. cit.*, pp. 205–42.

24 The fundamental work remains that of H. H. Schaeder, "Die islamische Lehre vom Vollkommenen Menschen, ihre Herkunft und dichterische Gestaltung," *Zeitschrift der Deutschen Morgenländischen Gesellschaft* 79 (1925), pp. 192–268.

25 Cf. A. Badawi, "L'humanisme dans la pensée arabe," *Studia Islamica* VI (1956), pp. 67–100.

its fundamental inspiration? Can one consider that the often suspect authors who professed it, like the authors of the Jâbir alchemical corpus, or Râzî, drew it from the Muslim religion? To take a precise example, it happens that Averroes let it be understood that religious ("divine") legislation must be judged according to its greater or lesser conformity to "human laws," that is to say, to the rules defining what regime is conformant to the ultimate end of man, such as is determined by philosophy and it alone. Thus, in a spectacular way, he turned inside out the point of view according to which the human laws must on the contrary be normed by the Divine Law.[26] Is this "humanism" the act of a good Muslim?

d) The question becomes difficult, but also interesting, under two conditions. First, the word "humanism" necessarily designates an attempt to accord man, vis-à-vis what he is not – including God – the status of an autonomic partner, a dignity that permits him to enter in a free relationship with his "others." Secondly, one must understand by "Islam," not a composite culture, but a religion such as is expressed in its normative documents. Now the scholars who deny the existence of this genre of humanism other than in Judaism and Christianity are not without authority, and their reasons merit being listened to.[27]

One can indeed take as argument the differences on the level of the representation of the origins of humanity and of the action of God toward it. In this respect, a nuance in the story of Adam is very revealing. In the Old Testament, it is

---

26 Cf. Averroës, *Commentary on Plato's Republic*, ed., intro., trans. and notes by E. I. J. Rosenthal, 3rd edition (Cambridge University Press, 1969), I, vii 11, p. 26, 16 ff and II, iii, 1, p. 63, 1. On the overturning of perspective, cf. S. Pinès, "On Averroes' Political Theory" *Studies in the History of Jewish Philosophy. The Transmission of Texts and Ideas* (in Hebrew) (Jerusalem: Mosad Bialiq, 1977), p. 92.

27 Cf. C. H. Becker, *op. cit.*, p. 34; Jörg Kraemer, *Das Problem der islamischen Kulturgeschichte* (Tübingen: Niemeyer, 1959), ch. VIII, pp. 35–40; Grunebaum, *Islam . . . , op. cit.*, p. 68.

Adam who names the things that God has not named, in particular, the animals:

> So from the soil Yahweh God fashioned all the wild animals and all the birds of heaven. These he brought to the man to see what he would call them; each one was to bear the name the man would give it.[28]

All at once, God takes the risk of having to learn something from man, and He confirms man's decisions, thus allowing him to act as legislator. According to the Koran, on the other hand, it is on the contrary God who names everything and teaches their names to Adam:

> And [the Lord] taught Adam all the names, then he had [the beings so named] parade before the Angels and He said [to the Angels]: "Advise me about the names of these beings here, if you are truthful."[29]

The superiority of man will thus be defined in relation to the angel, and it will be due to knowledge conferred by God. The idea according to which God could leave a region of liberty to man, wait for man's choice, and respect this choice, is thus removed. And with even greater reason, the idea of incarnation which, in Christianity, confers on man an incomparable dignity.

Though I do not want to enter deeply here into this vast debate, it is interesting to notice that the perhaps central difference between European humanism and what resembles it in the Arab world is also a consequence of the nature of the ancient texts that have been transmitted to the one and to the other. Ancient literature, in what it had of the truly "literary," that is, epic, tragic and lyric poetry, never reached the Arab world – unlike, as we have seen, philosophy and the ancient sciences. Now, it is just this literature that carried something

---

28 Genesis, 2:19; English trans., *The New Jerusalem Bible* (New York: Doubleday, 1985).

29 Koran, II, 31; French trans. Blachère, p. 736 ff. and note 29. The source seems to be *Bereshit Rabba*, 17, 4, ed. Theodor-Albeck, vol. 1, p. 155 ff.

like an ancient conception of man, with the models of his possible excellence in his affirmation in relation to the gods, to nature, to the city, etc. The Arab world has not therefore had to confront in its full force a global conception of man anterior to that of the Islamic religion: the idea of human excellence formed by the Arabs of the pagan "age of ignorance" (ğāhiliyya) had no weight in the face of the gravity of the Koranic message. Besides, the philosophical and scientific texts translated later did not express the pagan conception of man except under an attenuated form. The Christian world, on the other hand, had to measure itself against a more vigorous paganism: that of the anti-Christian Neo-Platonism of Porphyry and of Proclus that had not been adapted as the texts of Plotinus or Proclus translated into Arabic had been (like the *Theology of Aristotle, The Epistle on Divine Science,* or the *Discourse on the Pure Good* [*Liber de causis*]), and especially against that of the Greek tragedians, "the true adversaries of Christian sanctity."[30] Christianity therefore had to secrete more powerful antibodies.

Humanism with or without Renaissance

In the Arab world, any possible humanism has not, in any case, taken the form of "renaissances." This is another ambiguous term that must be clarified. Admittedly, nothing prevents the classification of certain periods of the intellectual history of the Muslim world under this convenient label. Thus, A. Mez (1869–1927) called the epoch of the Buyid Emirs in the tenth century the "Renaissance of Islam" – but as his book appeared posthumously, he could not explain the reasons for this appellation. Mez insisted on the importance of the penetration of sources, Greek and Christian, anterior and external to the Islamic religion, to explain its cultural devel-

---

30   Cf. H. U. von Balthasar, *Rechenschaft 1965*, Einsiedeln: Johannes, 1965, p. 24; Ph. Cormier, *op. cit.*, p. 99.

opment.[31] One then understands by "renaissance" a renewal
of intellectual studies made possible by a relative civil peace,
by the development and the diversification of the administration, and the subsequent emergence of a class with the leisure
necessary to devote themselves to the concerns of the spirit.
One could still consider as renaissances, in the eleventh century, the undertaking of a "revival of the religious sciences"
(*iḥyā' 'ulūm id-dīn*), the title of *al-Ghazālī's* great spiritual
encyclopaedia, or finally, the emergence of an Arabic national consciousness (*nahḍa*) at the end of the nineteenth century,
and even the movements that today are shaking up Islamic
civilization.

Is it not a question, in at least some of these phenomena,
of a return to the sources, and therefore of a "renaissance" in
the etymological sense of the term? Actually, it is often a question of a return to the sources of the Islamic religion itself, of
a desire to find again a more or less ideal purity: that of the
period of Medina when Mohammed himself organized his
community, that of the "well-guided" caliphs, before the
schisms that tore – and still divide – the Islamic religion at the
time of Ali. A reform movement that we might easily call
"modernist" could even give itself the paradoxical name of
salafiyya, that is to say, of fidelity to ancestral customs. These
returns all sought to go back to the sources, precisely, to the
origins of the Islamic religion. Europe presents analogous
cases, such as the successive reforms of the Church and, first
and foremost, the Franciscan movement that attempted to
revive the life led by the apostles of Christ.

But these phenomena, in the Islamic world as in Europe,
are not "renaissances" in the conceptual sense for which I
propose to reserve the word. It would be better to speak of
them as reawakenings or revivals. Indeed, one must note here

---

31 A. Mez, *Die Renaissance des Islams* (Heidelberg, 1922). Cf. the discussion
    in Joël Kraemer, *Humanism in the Renaissance of Islam. The Cultural
    Revival During the Buyid Age* (Leiden: Brill, 1986), pp. 1–5.

a fundamental difference. In one case, that of the religious awakenings, it is a matter of going back to the source while remaining in the interior of the tradition that it originated. In the other case, in contrast, that of renaissances properly said, the source one proposes to draw on is found beyond a solution of continuity, or even has never been in continuity with us. It is then a matter of *appropriating an origin in relation to which one feels foreign, and even alienated* – and in particular, the ancient sources.

Cultural Secondarity

This "Roman" attitude allows one to formulate what seems to me to constitute a special feature of European civilization. I am speaking here of a certain relation to cultural secondarity. I understand by this last term, in the first place, the banal fact that every culture is second. This is the case with every one that bears its stamp: even if it is acquired in earliest infancy, which makes it appear "entirely natural," culture is acquired and never innate. Besides, on the collective level, every culture is the heir of the one or several that preceded it. In this sense, every culture is a land of immigration. But there is more: cultural secondarity seems to me to have, in the case of Europe and of it alone, a supplementary dimension. Europe has indeed this special feature of having, one might say, *immigrated to itself.* I mean by this that the secondary character of the culture is not only present there as a fact, but is explicitly recognized and deliberately desired.

We have just characterized the history of European civilization, from the birth of Europe, as a nearly uninterrupted series of renaissances. Now, what is remarkable, as we have seen, is that the effort of returning back aims at something other than the cultural recoveries and religious revivals that traverse every civilization. This effort does not tend toward the primitive period; it is not a return toward what is proper to the culture and which would have existed in all its purity at the time of the founding origins. On the contrary, it tends toward a source located *outside* of European culture – in this case, in Greco-Latin antiquity. A hugely important example of this fact is Law, such as it was systematized from the "Papal Revolution" of the late Eleventh Century on. What the Bologna legists studied were not the legal rules that were actually enforced at their time, but ancient Roman law: "it was the body of law, the legal system, *of an earlier civilization* (my emphasis, R. B.) . . . that formed the object of Europe's first legal study." [32]

Let us recall here a massive social fact: for centuries, the European elites have been selected according to their capacity to assimilate ancient languages. One sometimes compares this system to that of ancient China, and in French student argot, one speaks of the great university dons as "mandarins." The analogy is tempting: there also, the mandarins were recruited through a literary competition. But one forgets the difference which is essential: the lettered Chinese were experts in *Chinese* letters; in Europe, on the contrary, one studied the classics of two *other* civilizations, and of an otherness that was sometimes painfully felt.

Husserl, in a famous conference in which Europe was an issue, spoke of what is "Greco-European." [33] The hyphen, that linking line, seems to me to pose, or conceal, as many problems as forming the adjective "Judeo-Christian." [34] It constitutes an implicit claim of continuity. As if the European were the sole heir of the Greek; as if, especially, the heritage had

---

32 H. J. Berman, *Law and Revolution. The Formation of the Western Legal Tradition* (Cambridge (Mass.): Harvard University Press, 1983), p. 122.

33 Husserl, "Die Krisis des europäischen Menschentums und die Philosophie," in *Die Krisis der europäischen Wissenschaften . . .* , Husserliana, vol. VI (The Hague: Nijhoff, 1962), pp. 314–48, cited on p. 329.

34 Cf. *supra.*, p. 43.

peaceably slid from one to the other, without rupture. Now, the contrary is in fact the truth. And it is the rupture that has revealed itself as fecund.

Two Cultures without Renaissances

One can get some idea of this by examining the case of two great civilizations, both quite respectable, but in which the phenomenon I have called, in the precise sense of the term, a "renaissance," never occurred.

Byzantium

The situation of secondarity in relation to the past aimed at by the "renaissances" is proper to Europe in the narrow sense as we have defined it. Thus, Byzantium never knew it. Admittedly, one does not have any trouble locating, in the cultural history of the Byzantine world, an uninterrupted "humanist" tradition. One sees there a series of "renaissances" follow one after the other, which constitute the counterpart, and often the model or a more or less direct motor, for analogous events occurring in Europe: the reestablishment of philological and literary studies in the ninth century with Photius or in the fourteenth with John Italus and Michael Psellus, and even a dream of Neo-Paganism in George Gemistus Plethon in the fifteenth century. But the great difference is that, for the Byzantine Greeks, Hellenism was considered as their proper past. Theodorus Metochites could still affirm: "We are the compatriots of the ancient Hellenes by race and by language."[35] For the Byzantines, it was only a matter of appropriating better and better what had always been their property.

---

35 Cited, without references, by C. Diehl, *Etudes Byzantines* . . . (Paris: Picard, 1905), p. 398.

I could not express the situation and its consequences better than an Austrian historian of Byzantine art, who wrote:

> One calls these epochs during which one turns in an intense way toward the ancient heritage "renaissances," and one has compared them to the renaissances and the "recoveries" of Western Europe, both rightly and wrongly. Quite rightly, because in the renaissances in the West and at Byzantium, the intention and the direction in which one went were similar. But also wrongly, because the Occidental renaissances were of shorter duration, of less intensity, and separated from each other by intervals during which the tendency went entirely in the opposite direction. The Byzantine renaissances, conversely, followed nearly without a resolution of continuity, they were only nodal points on which forces were concentrated and efforts were almost always there. This is why one is right to speak of a "permanent renaissance" in Byzantium. But as a consequence these concentrations lacked tendencies that aimed at just what characterizes an authentic renaissance: Antiquity was for the Byzantines something so near that it could not establish that feeling of estrangement which would drive creation [schöpferisches Fremdheitserlebnis] and so nothing could truly be "reborn."[36]

Islam

In the lands of Islamic faith there were some attempts to restore a knowledge perceived as having come from outside, and moreover, very explicitly and technically identified under the name of "external sciences" – as opposed to the

---

36 O. Demus, "Die Rolle der byzantinischen Kunst in Europa," *Jahrbuch der Österreichischen Byzantinischen Gesellschaft* 14 (1965), pp. 139–55, cited on p. 141.

"traditional sciences" grouped around the Koran and what facilitates exegesis (grammar, poetry, etc). One comes across just these sorts of attempts in the period when books treating these "external sciences" were translated.

Thus, Al-Farabi presented a schema of the history of the transmission of philosophic and scientific knowledge that presupposed this effort: the knowledge passed from the Chaldeans, ancient inhabitants of Iraq, to the Arabs by way of the Egyptians, the Greeks, and the Syrians (Christians). Moreover, Al-Farabi associated the possession of internal rules of philosophical practice with the political art permitting its restoration if it should happen to be lost or corrupted.[37] Everything leads one to believe that he conceived of his own activity as preparing a restoration of philosophy after its eclipse.

One could equally cite, also in the philosophical domain, the effort of Averroes to restore Aristotelian thought to what he believed to be its authenticity by commenting systematically on his works. He considered that Aristotle's work had been corrupted by Avicenna in a Neo-Platonic direction, which represented, however, a previous reception of the same thought. But the work of Averroes had hardly any offspring in the land of its origin, Andalusia and Morocco, or in general in the southern Mediterranean. Nothing in any event that merits comparison to the enormous reception that it knew north of the Mediterranean, first in the Jewish communities, and then among Christians.

---

37 Farabi, *Taḥṣīl aṣ-Ṣaʿāda*, ed. *Yā Sīn, Dār al-Andaloss* (Beirut, 1983), §65, p. 97, or the English trans. of M. Mahdi, *Alfarabi's Philosophy of Plato and Aristotle* (Cornell University Press, 1969), IV, §63, p. 50. On the Greek origin of the philosophy of the Arabs, cf. *Kitāb al-Ḥurūf*, II, §156, ed. M. Mahdi, (Beirut: *Dār al-Machreq*, 1969), p. 159. Cf. my "Eorum praeclara ingenia. Conscience de la nouveauté et prétention à la continuité chez Farabi et Maïmonide," in D. Mallet, ed., *Etudes de philosophie arabe*, Actes du colloque de Bordeaux, June 17–19, 1994, *Bulletin d'études orientales* XLVIII (1996), pp. 87–102.

These sorts of attempts never continued over a very long period of time. They came up short, and the "traditional sciences" remained more or less alone in the lists, after the Sunni normalization in the eleventh century. Intellectual life exhausted itself by a refusal or incapacity to open up to new sources. One might then jokingly suggest a parallel to the theory of M. Lombard on the medieval Muslim world economy, which was fettered by the exhaustion, or rather the non-renewal, of internal natural resources.

Unless we will have to propose, on the contrary, a hypothesis on the whole of the cultural decline of the Muslim world, which could be placed in line with what I am trying to show here. According to this hypothesis, the cultural stagnation of the Islamic world (which besides must be nuanced, according to time and the place) would paradoxically be due, not to a rejection but, on the contrary, to an excess of assimilation. The Islamic world would have ceased to advance from not having been able to maintain a relationship of externality to the sources from which it borrowed, and precisely because they were absorbed. If one may be permitted to reuse the somewhat baroque image of the ass before which one hangs an unattainable lure, it has swallowed the carrot which made it advance. A hypothesis of this genre has in any event been suggested with regard to the history of the sciences:

> The final result of all this is an instrumentalist and religiously oriented view of all secular and permitted knowledge.... The decline of science occurred, not in the context of opposition (as is usually thought) but in the context of acceptance and assimilation ... – that is, it set in when the sciences came to be accepted and practiced only to the extent that they were legitimated by the instrumentalist view.[38]

---

38 Cf. A. I. Sabra, "The Appropriation and Subsequent Naturalization of Greek Science in Medieval Islam: a Preliminary Statement," *History of Science* XXV (1987), pp. 223–43, especially p. 240.

Funded Scholars and Parvenus

Conversely, European culture, taken as a whole, is an effort to go back to a past that was never its own, but in relation to which there was something like an irreparable fall, a painfully perceived "estrangement." It is not necessary to pause here to consider in what way this vision of the past is artificial. I am not unaware that what has come down to us of ancient culture is the result of a work of selection practiced since the Alexandrian period, and that the image we have created for ourselves of its totality generalizes excessively in imagining an "ancient world" entirely at the level of its masterpieces. I am not unaware either, in the inverse sense, that the presence of monuments and of ancient texts in the European space, and especially in Italy, assured a minimum of continuity despite everything. But what is alone decisive for me is the consciousness taken of the situation. Now, for the Europeans, it is a consciousness of being latecomers, and of having to go back to a source that "we" are not and which has never been "us."

This consciousness is vivid from the beginning of the European project. It is even, perhaps, the motor of its history. The figure of Charlemagne, whom one nicknamed "the father of Europe" (*Pater Europae*),[39] can serve as a paradigm here. This parvenu dreamed of competing with Byzantium, in comparison with which, despite its then-weakened state, he could not help but feel inferior. Byzantium had all the signs of legitimacy: material riches ("the gold of Byzantium"), a dynasty, the Roman name (the second Rome), manuscripts and scholars to read them, and numerous saints' relics that were signs of the continuity of the Church from its apostolic foundation.

---

39 In the epic "Karolus et Leo papa," ln. 504; Monumenta Germaniae Historica, Poet. I, 1 (1881), 379. I cite following K.-F. Werner, *Karl der Große oder Charlemagne. Von der Aktualität einer überholten Fragestellung* (Munich, 1995), p. 4.

In his biography of Charlemagne, Einhard recounts that the emperor had bequeathed three tables of silver and one of gold in his will. On the first were represented, respectively, the maps of Constantinople and of Rome, and a map of the entire world.[40] One will note that two maps are conspicuous by their absence: among maps of cities, that of Aachen, the capital of the Carolingian Empire. This city must at that time cut a poor figure alongside the two reference points which Europe never ceased ogling, the two Romes, the ancient and the contemporary. But also missing was the map of Europe, the newly founded empire of the Occident. Its founder could not gaze at himself complacently in the image of his creation.

Europe had to be included, of course, in the map of the world. But this was the world before Columbus, without the New World, and all the more without Oceania. The geographical center was somewhere in the Middle East. The religious center was, for the Muslims, in Mecca, and for the Jews and the Christians, in Jerusalem. The center of culture was, for the Arabs, at Baghdad, and for the Christians, at Byzantium. It was not, in any event, in what was beginning to be called "Europe." Charlemagne could thus see the place his own Occidental empire occupied, far from the centers, far from Jerusalem, far from everything – eccentric.

He tried to be linked to Byzantium first by competing with it, and even in aping it – in architecture, for example: the basilica of Aachen imitates that of Ravenna, the single accessible example of Byzantine architecture. Then, by trying to intervene in the theological debates – for example, on icons, with the *Libri Carolini*. Finally, to the great scandal of the Basileus, he dared to have himself crowned emperor of the Occident. All of this rested on an admission and a recognition: legitimacy was elsewhere, it came from elsewhere, it was nec-

---

40 I am citing from the commodious little edition of Einhard, *Vita Karoli Magni / Das Leben Karls des Grossen*, Lateinisch /Deutsch, ed. E. S. Firchow (Stuttgart: Reclam, 1981), §33, p. 66 ff.

essary to have it come from elsewhere – possibly under the form of Byzantine princesses whose blood would improve that of the Carolingian heirs. As is known, politically speaking, the Carolingian project failed. At the most it fed, with hardly any possible resolution of continuity, a persistent dream of restoration. One can thus summarize the history of Europe as being that of a *translatio imperii*.[41]

More profoundly, the feeling of legitimacy of the Occidental empire remained fragile, to the point that a certain feeling of bastardy arose from time to time, even in the Occident. It was the case, for example, with Luther who, once Charles V banned him from the empire, used it as grist for his mill by contesting the legitimacy of the Occidental Empire which, according to Luther, had usurped titles valid only for Byzantium.[42] The feeling of cultural inferiority in relation to Byzantium remained quite vivid even after Charlemagne.[43]

On the other hand, the fundamental attitude that made European cultural history possible is precisely Charlemagne's. The same biographer, Einhard, tells how Charlemagne used to keep tablets and a stylus under his pillow to slog away at writing when he couldn't sleep.[44] The father of Europe was illiterate, but he was learning to write. He who, from our images at Epinal, was the father of schools was in fact himself a schoolboy, and the sort who took night classes. Such was the making of Europe: taking after its "father," it is an illiterate continent that learned to read – not Gaulish or German, etc. – but Latin and Greek.

---

41 Cf. P. Sloterdijk, *Falls Europa erwacht. Gedanken zum Programm einer Weltmacht am Ende des Zeitalters ihrer politischen Absence* (Frankfurt: Suhrkamp, 1994), p. 34 ff.

42 *An Open Letter to the Christian Nobility of the German Nation. . .* , no. 26 (added in the second edition, 1520), *Works of Martin Luther*. (Philadelphia: Muhlenberg Press, 1943), vol. 2, p. 153–158.

43 Cf. M. Rentschler, "Griechische Kultur und Byzanz im Urteil westlicher Autoren des 10. Jahrhunderts," *Saeculum* 29 (1978), pp. 324–55.

44 Einhard, *Life of Charlemagne*, cited ed., §25, p. 48 ff.

One is familiar with the distinction dear to Charles Maurras between the heir and the funded scholar, a comparison that, in his spirit, was to the advantage of the former. The latter, an uncouth drudge, whose successes were only scholarly, could never compete with the heir. Had the heir not had from the cradle, even received from his ancestral line, an innate knowledge? He accomplished with ease what cost the scholar a thousand efforts that were often clumsy, always lacking grace. If the scholar "arrived," he betrayed his modest origins in a thousand ways – gestures, turns of phrase, tastes – and would always remain a parvenu. Can we apply here something conceived about individuals to the level of civilizations? Europe is entirely a continent of scholars, of parvenus, of grinds (in Latin!). That is its greatness.

An Inverse Adoption

One can accordingly characterize the cultural history of Europe as being that of an inverse adoption.[45] Usually, it is the parents who adopt the child, either from their incapacity to have one themselves or because those they have had have proved unable to play the role they expected of them. Thus, we find Roman emperors adopting adults as their successor. In Europe, the process has functioned in the other direction. Those who came later chose their ancestors for themselves. The European heritage is the object of a vast usurpation of a legacy. The Europeans are the heirs of antiquity in nothing. At the very least, they are not, if it is necessary as in most cases to understand by "heir," someone who has only taken "the trouble to be born," and who has received from the cradle all material and cultural goods, which his parents have left him. They are heirs, on the other hand, if one conceives of the fact of being an heir as nothing more than an activity of appropriation.

---

45 I realized that the idea is already to be found in H. J. Berman, *op. cit.,* p. 3.

An entire literary genre, in the contemporary Occident, does everything to reconstitute the genealogy of our modernity. This genealogy is taken in a paradoxical sense: indeed, it is no longer a matter of proving one's nobility by exhibiting an uninterrupted line of glorious ancestors; on the contrary, it is a matter of denouncing bastardy, of denouncing an impure origin. This is the sense that the term has taken, at least since Rousseau,[46] or in any event, certainly since Nietzsche attempted to write *The Genealogy of Morals*. There are then some people who, applying the genealogical method to the historical reality of Europe, do their utmost to show the illegitimacy of its descent. They do it either in comparison to one or another civilization considered as the source (classical Greece or Rome), in comparison to another civilization considered as an equally legitimate heir, such as Islam, or yet again in comparison to one considered even more legitimate, such as Byzantium.

These people admittedly are right about the facts, and I have besides given some arguments to shore up this idea. But they do not see that their enterprise destroys itself: believing to unmask the misery of Europe, they on the contrary present evidence of the secret of its greatness. Because, when all is said and done, the cultural poverty of Europe has been her good fortune. It obliged it to work and to borrow. On the contrary, the richness of Byzantium paralyzed it, got in its way, because it had no need to look elsewhere. This has been noticed in regard to the history of art.[47] One noticed it equally in regard to philosophy:

---

46   Cf. Rousseau, *Lettre à C. de Beaumont* (1763) in *Œuvres complètes*, collection L'intégrale (Paris: Seuil, 1971), vol. 3, p. 340b.

47   Cf. A. Grabar, "L'asymétrie des relations de Byzance et de l'Occident dans le domaine des arts au Moyen Age" in *Byzanz und der Westen. Studien zur Kunst des europäischen Mittelalters*, ed. I. Hutter (Vienna: Verlag der österreichischen Akademie der Wissenschaften, 1984), pp. 9–24.

> As speakers of Greek, the Byzantine world remained closed to the philosophical culture of the Islamic lands; its intellectual richness, its tradition, its heritage made it unnecessary for it to look elsewhere. The Latin world, on the contrary, was philosophically poor, and its poverty served as an opening. . . . The good fortune of the Latin speaking Occidental world was thus in its lack of philosophical culture which obliged it to make some meaning out of its problems rather than with instruments.[48]

The fact is that Byzantium has never experienced the need to borrow from the Arab world, in any event, in the philosophical domain. There was no intellectual "racism" behind that: Byzantium translated Arabic doctors, as for example, the treatises of Razi on smallpox – probably at the moment when an epidemic had reduced the doctors of pure Greek background to silence.[49] But it seems that Byzantium never knew Farabi, Avicenna, or Averroes. Or rather, if it knew them, it was, surprisingly, from translations of the works of Saint Thomas Aquinas, completed in the fourteenth century, in which the doctrines of the two latter thinkers were expounded and criticized.

The consciousness that Europe had of having its sources outside of itself had the consequence of displacing its cultural identity, such that it has no other identity than an *eccentric identity*.

It is now fashionable to hurl at European culture the adjective "eurocentric." To be sure, every culture, like every living being, can't help looking at the other ones from its own vantage point, and Europe is no exception. Yet, no culture

---

48 A. de Libera, *La philosophie médiévale* (Paris: Presses Universitaires de France, 1993), p. 309 and p. 262.

49 Cf. M.-H. Congourdeau, "Le traducteur grec du traité de Rhazès sur la variole," *Storia e ecdotica dei testi medici greci*, ed. A. Garzya, Atti del 2 convegno internazionale, Paris, May 24–26, 1994 (Naples, 1996), pp. 99–111.

was ever so little centered on itself and so interested in the other ones as Europe. China saw itself as the "Middle Kingdom." Europe never did. "Eurocentrism" is a misnomer. Worse: it is the contrary of the truth.

VII
The Improper Proper

Looking for what is proper to European culture, as I am in the process of doing, is not an enterprise that one can carry off without precautions owing to the very nature of this research. Indeed, even the word "proper" has equivocal connotations. It designates, in French at least, both the contrary of dirty and that of improper; and it may be that these two senses have a profound relation.[1] In any event, the reference to what is proper to a culture can invite the exclusion of what is not that culture – as a "dirty" stranger. Now, the model of relation to oneself and to the other that I propose here seems to me to make, on the level of principles, any attitude of this sort impossible. It equally nips in the bud, it seems to me, other cultural perversions. Before showing how this is the case, however, let us first recall what specific relation Europe has to culture.

My Culture as an Other

This specific relation is a consequence of the phenomenon of cultural secondarity, and as such it takes on in Europe the intensity that we have seen. Culture cannot be, for the European, something that he possesses and that constitutes his identity. It will be on the contrary something fundamen-

---

1   J. Derrida, *L'écriture et la différence* (Paris: Seuil, 1967), p. 272.

tally strange, that therefore makes an effort of appropriation necessary. It is only by way of a detour through the anterior and the strange that the European reaches what is proper to him.[2]

As a consequence, one will refrain from returning to the Greek, Latin, or Jewish cultural treasures with satisfaction, as if it were a matter of guaranteed income justifying the laziness of the possessor, as to make "the rounds of the owner in the garden of the past." One can admire, and rightly so, Greek rationality and democracy, Roman order, the Jewish sense of transcendence, etc. But their enumeration, already annoying as a cliché, becomes suspect when it is a matter of attributing them to ourselves with self-satisfaction. Thus one has heard a Soviet diplomat, searching for a justification of the anti-Chinese policy of the U.S.S.R., becoming teary-eyed over the sources of Occidental culture: "the treasure and prerogative of our Occidental Christian civilization . . . ; you and I have been nourished on the same sources . . . Greece! Christianity!"[3]

European culture can in fact never, in the strictest terms, be "mine," since it is none more than a route to travel along indefinitely which leads to a foreign source. One should not speak, with W. R. Gibbons, of "our beautiful Occidental civilization."[4] But it is important to locate the error precisely: it is true to say that this civilization is "beautiful," and even "admirable"; what is false, on the other hand, is to believe that it is "ours." The culture is not an origin peaceably possessed, but an end conquered in hard-fought struggle.

It is necessary then to return from the derived sense of the word "culture," that which I employed up until now for reasons of convenience, to the original sense, the *cultura animi* of

---

2   Cf. Hölderlin, letter of the 4th of December, 1801 to Böhlendorff; *Grosse Stuttgarter Ausgabe*, VI–1, p. 425 ff.

3   S. Leys, *Ombres chinoises* (Paris: Union générale d'éditions, 1974), p. 267.

4   Hergé, *Le lotus bleu*, Casterman, p. 7.

the Latins.[5] It is even appropriate, perhaps, to protest against an unwarranted extension of this meaning, one that would call "culture" whatever way of behaving one has received from one's ancestors and the prevailing environment.

Of the Good Use of Authenticity

For Europe, the source is what is external. There lies the possibility. For it is unhealthy to recall one's proper glorious past, to recall a glorious past *that is one's own.* A reflection of this genre cannot avoid fomenting resentment that will turn alternately toward oneself and toward others, and that will have paralyzing effects. For if what was great was already myself, it will be necessary for me to ask myself why I have fallen in relation to that greatness. To avoid morose soul searching, one will be tempted to find these reasons outside, in the malice of one or another "other." The accusation of the exterior permits one to turn away from the internal causes that are, however, the only causes one can treat. Thus, one is saved the difficult effort regarding oneself such a treatment would require.

And so, for example, to speak only of the civilizations that have been touched on here, the Arab world has known a period of regression for several centuries, or at least of relative stagnation, clearly a decline in comparison to the splendors of ninth-century Baghdad. Often, it blames the Turks, guilty of having reestablished a strict Sunni orthodoxy, then the Mongols, guilty of having destroyed Baghdad in 1258, then Occidental colonization – or even the Jews. The Byzantine civilization provides another example; it lost its political power, up to and including its capital which gave it its name. Its heirs accuse their hereditary enemy, the Turks, but also the Latins, capable of a "knife in the back" as during the Fourth Crusade (1204). It's exactly in virtue of the same logic that many sensibilities in the Occident function today. The French accuse the

---

5   Cf. Cicero, *Tusculan Disputations* II, 5, 13.

Anglo-Saxons for the loss of the domination that their language exerted on European culture. The Europeans on the whole will throw the blame for unemployment or the insecurity of their neighborhoods on the presence of non-indigenous immigrants. Occidentals, Europeans and Americans alike will seek out those responsible for the relative fall in their share of the world market by accusing the Japanese and the "four dragons," etc.

If the model to imitate must be exterior, the greatness to recall must be that of the other. The evocation of past grandeurs seems to me to be a sane remedy or a dangerous poison, according to whether it is applied to oneself or another. For example, Occidental scholars who sing the praises of Islamic civilization at its apogee, of its scientific advances, of what one calls its "tolerance," or alternately, the praises of the intellectual and artistic refinement of Medieval Byzantium, are no doubt animated by the very laudable feeling of an injustice to set right. It may be, however, that the result is contrary to the end desired, and that they encourage, on the part of those who consider themselves the heirs of these civilizations, nostalgic dreams that at bottom are somewhat debilitating. On the other hand, the recall of the past grandeurs of Islam or Byzantium – not to mention those of India or China – is among the most salutary for Europe itself, as it encourages it to view itself with at least some modesty.

For Some Table Manners in Cultural Cannibalism

One can apply the same remarks in a negative key. A culture's past is never entirely rosy. Innocent civilizations exist only in the dreams of those – whether they belong to them or not – who know them poorly. This is true for Europe's past as well. It is even more valid for Europe, because its relations with the rest of the world, since the Renaissance, have been relations of conquest and occupation. One must then ask how one knows what to do with this past. It's not contemporary Germany alone but all of Europe that has a problem to "come to terms with its past" (*Vergangenheitsbewältigung*). And it is to Europe's honor that it has historians who recall what this past has truly been with ever greater precision and less indulgence.

It would be far too easy to dismiss the question by reminding others of the negative aspects they might find in their own past if only they looked well. The "no, you!" remains infantile, even between civilizations. It is just as infantile to suspect that malice, and even plotting, is always at the origin of catastrophes. Thus, for example, the demographic collapse of the pre-Columbian societies at the moment of the conquest was not caused only by the suppression of the Indian revolts. We would be better inspired to take into account more sobering objective causes, whether they be conscious, such as the superiority of weaponry, or involuntary, such as misunderstandings . . . or the introduction of more virulent strains of microbes. However, one must confront the past without letting a paralyzing guilt, which would prevent even the repair of what can be repaired, contaminate repentance.

Hegel noted one day that we act like savages who kill their old parents.[6] Franz von Baader specified somewhere what we do to them: "all men are naturally anthropophagi." We understand that every culture nourishes itself on those that preceded it. Yet one must still know how to behave at the table. Now, it is in this point of view remarkable that Europe has drawn from this perhaps inevitable cannibalism, in which it has behaved no better than any other powerful civilization, something productive of critical reflection about itself. Usually, a culture reflects on itself when it is constrained by an inferior situation. One has examples of this wherever Europeans have intervened in external civilizations and, without modifying them with a massive influx of people,

---

6   Hegel, *Jenenser Realphilosophie*, ed. Hoffmeister (Hamburg: Meiner, 1967), p. 202, nt. 3.

have constrained them to open up. One can think of the
reforms of the Ottoman Empire after the defeat of its navy at
Lepanto (1571), or after the failure of the siege of Vienna
(1683), or yet again, in Japan, of the Meiji reforms that
appeared after the forced opening of the ports bombarded by
Commodore Perry (1854).

Europe, on the other hand, presents the perhaps unique
case of self-reflection brought about through its relation to
peoples that it has just vanquished, whose lands it just conquered. It resulted in a prolonged attempt to see itself
through the eyes of the other. The *Persian Letters* of
Montesquieu or the *Cartas marruecas* of Cadalso are thus an
exclusively European phenomenon. The literary genre these
works represent, and to which one can add the entire myth of
the "noble savage," is in fact the somewhat bastardized transposition of more profound reflections whose first occasion
was without any doubt the discovery of America. One is
familiar with the reflections of Montaigne on the Indians in
the famous essay "On Cannibals."[7] And the extrapolations by
men of letters were founded on the immense treasure of first-
hand observations amassed by the missionaries. Just think of
the immense success of the *Edifying and Curious Letters*. The
external defeat of the "others" was turned around, in the eyes
of these thinkers, into a victory: Europe tried to see itself
through the eyes of the stranger, and therefore not as self-evident, nor that it constituted necessarily the only possible, and
even less the best possible of solutions to the human problem.
One may wonder why Europe, and it alone, engaged in this
reflexive adventure which overtook the colonial epic: it was
because Europe already had within itself, in its constitutive
relation to the classical sources, everything that was necessary
to feel inferior.

---

7 Montaigne, *Essais*, I, 31; cf. Ferran Sáez i Mateu, "Michel de Montaigne.
   Dels caníbals. Estudi preliminar, traducció i anotació crítica," *Anuari de
   la Societat catalana de filosofia* V (Barcelona, 1992–93), pp. 87–143.

Cultural Identity?

The precision of vocabulary required above in regard to the word "culture" is not simply purist. Indeed, it implies that one submits the widespread expression of "cultural identity" to a deeper examination. And in particular, that one ask oneself in what sense what one understands most often by it merits respect.

To rise up to

If the word "culture" refers, in conformity with its original sense, to the personal effort to ennoble the spirit in elevating oneself to a classical model, it indicates an enrichment of the identity of the one who accepts taking on himself such an effort. In this case, the cultural identity merits receiving a little of that respect which, in the strongest sense, the person alone can deserve. It will be, besides, because the culture will have been integrated by the person that culture will have become like a person. On the other hand, it often happens that one uses the term "culture" to designate rather the weight of belonging, the ballast of everything that is not chosen but endured. In which case, one can feel at the most a polite sympathy for that culture, but never true respect. One will be able to respect, not the culture itself, but the people who are the carriers of it, and rather despite it than because of it. In the inverse sense, the affirmation of a "cultural identity" of this sort could be an excusable reaction, especially if it comes from a minority who, lost in the midst of a heterogeneous mass, feels menaced by it. But no culture is allowed to claim the dignity that belongs to the person. And it happens that this dignity must be defended against a culture that harasses it, and against the temptation of finding one's "roots" – that is to say, as suggested implicitly by the image, of regressing toward the stupid immobility of the vegetable.

This deserves some respect

Just letting your culture happen

In a word, one must distinguish what is "ours" and what is good. The proper is not necessarily the good. It is already shocking to say *my country, right or wrong*. The same formula, applied to what each calls "his culture," produces equally perverse effects. As a Frenchman, I pride myself on being the offspring of a nation of traitors: the Gauls, who were sufficiently intelligent to permit having their "authenticity" torn from them – with among others, the charming custom of human sacrifice – to the benefit of Roman civilization.

The Interest of Disinterestedness

As the sources of European culture are not "us," nothing invites us to restrain their study to the "Occidentals" that we are. Thus, the distance between us and the ancient Greeks is not, in principle, less than that which separates them from other modern cultures. The deepening of our knowledge of the Greeks leads equally well, on the level of the individual as on that of the entire scientific community, to becoming at the same time acutely conscious of their strangeness. For the modern European to appropriate them to himself he would require a disappropriation of himself that is fundamentally just as great as it would be for an African or Chinese. In this way, to study the classics is in no way to occidentalize oneself. The California campuses recently resounded with slogans that aimed to translate political demands in favor of minorities into university programs. It was necessary to balance out, and even to replace the study of male authors of the white race with writers of the female sex and/or of color. This attitude cannot not be fomented, as the offense demands vengeance, out of an unwarranted demand for the exclusivity of the ancient heritage on the part of the modern Occident. The two are obverse and reverse of the same (counterfeit) coin.

It is not therefore a matter of suggesting the study of classic works to those people called non-European because their comprehension would permit a better understanding of the Occident – which is, besides, entirely true. But on a deeper level, it is more a matter of getting them to realize that, for "them" just as for "us," these works are, quite simply, capable of interesting them. The question of knowing what classics it is necessary to read, or, even, of knowing what authors must be considered as classics, has nothing to do with their belonging or not to the tradition whose heirs we feel ourselves to be. Would it be better to study Sophocles or Kalidasa, Homer or the *Edda*, Plato or Confucius? The best thing, if it were a question of deciding between authors from two different traditions, would perhaps be to ask a representative of a third tradition what seems the most enriching for him. But the sole definitive criterion is that of internal interest. The question should never be one of knowing if an author belongs to our tradition or not, and yet less if he has the same sex or the same "race" as we do. The only legitimate question seeks to know whether an author is worth the trouble of being read for himself.

This is, besides, just what the Europeans themselves have done in the past. They have not studied the Greek and Latin classics because they were the sources of Europe, and therefore because they were fundamentally themselves, so that in studying them they came to know themselves better, and were better able to affirm their own particularity. To the contrary, they studied them, as they studied besides Muslim or Jewish thinkers, because they found their works true, beautiful, interesting, etc. One could thus extract something like a cultural law according to which the appropriation of a source is fruitful only if it is disinterested. In stark terms: only what is free pays.

In the same way, in the religious domain, faith does not produce its effects except where it remains faith, and not calculation. The civilization of Christian Europe has been constructed by people for whom the end was not at all to construct a "Christian civilization," but to make the most of the consequences of their faith in Christ. We owe it to people who believe in Christ, not to people who believe in Christianity. These people were Christians, and not what one might call "Christianizers." A good example of this is furnished by Pope

Gregory the Great.[8] His reform laid the foundations for the European Middle Ages. Now, he believed that the end of the world was very near, an end that to his mind would remove the space in which any "Christian civilization" might establish itself. What he constructed, and what would last a good millennium, was in his eyes only an entirely provisional marching order, a way of setting in order a house one was soon going to leave. Inversely, those who propose as the primary end of their actions the "saving of the Christian Occident" have to be careful not to deploy practices that, as we have had examples of, are located outside of what Christian ethics, not to mention the most elementary common moral order, authorizes.

A Parable

In this way, the question of the cultural identity of Europe cannot be posed in an independent fashion. It is indissolubly tied to the question of the relation of Europe to other civilizations, anterior and/or exterior to it. For Europe, the relationship to oneself exists in relation to the other. Nothing can better illustrate this, it seems to me, than a sort of parable that I will borrow from an author prior to Christianity, in order to bring out an aspect of the European experience that is not explained by it. The story is from Herodotus.[9] Darius, the king of Persia, sought to show that custom (*nomos*) rules over all men, or if one prefers, that everything is conventional, by basing his argument on how men consider their own practices to be the best. Now these practices are at loggerheads with each other, for what is practiced by some is an abomination for others. To show it, Darius brought together some Greeks and

---

8   Cf. all of the third section, "Eschatology," of C. Dagens, *Grégoire le Grand. Culture et expérience chrétienne* (Paris: Etudes augustiniennes, 1977).

9   Herodotus, *Inquiries* III, 38, 3. I have taken my inspiration here from S. Benardete, *Herodotean Inquiries* (La Haye: Nijhoff, 1969), p. 80 ff.

some representatives of a tribe from India, and asked the two groups about their funeral customs and their willingness to change. The Greeks who, at that time, incinerated their dead, explained that they would not eat them at any price. The Indians, who devoured their cadavers, cried that they would not burn theirs for anything in the world. The two groups seem to be on the same level. Such is, in any event, the conclusion of Darius, and tacitly, that of Herodotus.

Two characteristics, however, distinguished the Greeks: first, they listened in silence to the question of the king and they answered calmly, while the Indians bombarded him with their indignant cries and demanded that Darius keep silent. Second, the Greeks understood, by the intermediary of an interpreter, what one asked the Indians. In this way, the Greeks could be as attached to their particular practices – we would say, to their authenticity – as are the other peoples. But they accepted at least to become aware of the contingent character of their particularity, to open up to the rest of the world. In this way, the other cultures are translatable and susceptible to being raised to the universal by language. The anonymous interpreter is here the symbol of what Herodotus himself never stopped doing in his *Inquiries*: to interpret the rest of the known world for the Greeks. On the level of funeral practices, this elevation to the universal found besides its image in incineration, by which the body, which is what singularizes us, finds itself abolished. On the other hand, ingestion symbolizes an indissoluble attachment to what is proper to us.

The attitude that Herodotus illustrated was far from being the rule in ancient Greece. But it is the rule that Europe took over. Europe has given it more weight with the value its religion placed on secondarity. It remains valid as a program of a certain relation of Europe to what is proper to it: a relationship open to the universal. One can formulate it by reusing, even if it must be nuanced, a famous pun of Ortega y Gasset. Recently returned from America, he had answered someone who asked him the reasons for his return: *"Europa es el único continente que tiene un contenido.*" "Europe is a continent / container [Castilian doesn't distinguish the two words] that has a content, and it is the only one to have one." The formula seems overly proud. It was perhaps for Ortega. For me, if one understands it well, it is completely the contrary. For one must equally realize that "to have a content" supposes, rightly, that one can "have" a content, and therefore that one "is" not this content, that one is not completely identified with it. One can thus reverse the formula: the content of Europe, it is just to be a container, to be open to the universal.

It is the same with Europe, on the level of civilization, as it is on the level of the individual, with the proper names of those who inhabit it. Our first names are, in the overwhelming majority of cases, names of people. Exceptions are rare, for example, adjectives (Constant, etc.). One sees here, besides, a concrete result of cultural secondarity: the Jewish and pagan proper names, which may have a meaning in Hebrew (John, etc.), in Latin (Mark, etc.) or in German (Bernard, etc.), have all been reused by the Christians, but their primitive sense has been forgotten. In the great majority of civilizations, names have a meaning – obviously laudatory – *a priori*, that indicates straightaway what one expects of the child so named. The European, on the other hand, possesses his identity only as an empty frame that he will have the task of filling in.

Europeanization for the Whole World

If such is the case, it is necessary to consider anew the problem of the relation between Europe and the rest of the world. Most of the time, one poses it in opposing these two terms in a simple way: the first designates what is already European, the second what is not. What is non-European can either seek to become it, or refuse to do this, accepting or rejecting what one will then call "Europeanization." In every scenario, one assumes that the other regions of the world have to adapt themselves to what already exists somewhere. To "Europeanize" oneself would therefore be to imitate Europe, which it is presumed is of course already European. This is what the philosophers do who use the concept of "Europeanization" and reflect on it. They are besides not very numerous.[10]

I would like to maintain here the opposite thesis, which may seem somewhat paradoxical, even if fundamentally it does no more than to take seriously Husserl's characterization of Europe as an "immanent teleology," an "entelechy" – and therefore for the human type that corresponds to it, as an infinite task, as infinite as the philosophical project.[11] Europe, I say, is nothing other than a constant movement of self-Europeanization. Europeanization is a movement internal to Europe; and moreover, it is the movement that constitutes Europe as such. Europe does not pre-exist Europeanization; Europe is the result of Europeanization, and is not its cause.

This thesis results directly from what has been shown earlier:[12] from the point of view of the historian, Europe has never been a space defined from the outset, preexisting, and in whose interior a certain culture would have developed. This was the case of America or Australia, cases that are fairly easy to isolate – because they are, actually, gigantic islands. And because they were, so to speak, given in a single blow, or nearly so, to the discoverers that gave them their names. Europe, on the other hand, lacking convincing natural frontiers, is not a definite space, but a space that defines itself, in detaching itself from the rest of the world. The moment one

---

10 I am thinking especially about Joachim Ritter, in some reflections that touch especially on Turkey. Cf. "Europäisierung als europäisches Problem" (1956) in *Metaphysik und Politik. Studien zu Aristoteles und Hegel*, 2nd ed. (Frankfurt: Suhrkamp [stw 199], 1988), pp. 321–40.

11 Cf. "Die Krisis des europäischen Menschentums und die Philosophie," *op. cit.* pp. 319, 347, 320, 338 ff.

12 Cf. *supra.*, ch. I, p. 6.

began to call a cultural entity "Europe," and not a direction (west, the direction of the setting sun) is the moment that this region cut itself off from Byzantium and from the Islamic world, partly because of a separation come from the outside, partly because of a more or less conscious effort to make something new. The south of the Mediterranean had been separated from the north by the Arab conquest of its southern shores, and therefore by an external event; but the resistance to this was the effect of an internal will. The western Christendom had been separated from the east first of all as a consequence of external factors: a difference of languages and of cultures, then of too-important delays in communication, factors that were perceived very early on. But the decision to recreate an Occidental empire is, on the part of Charlemagne and the Papacy, an internal decision, due in part to the desire to thwart the Byzantine Empire.

The same consequence can be drawn from the examination of Europe as a civilization: its sources are external to it. Its profane culture is, in the last analysis, of Greek origin; its religion is of Jewish origin. We have seen that the consciousness of this externality surfaces sometimes. According to an already ancient image, there are two cities that classically symbolize its roots: "Athens" and "Jerusalem." Now, what is less often noticed is that neither of these two cities belong to the space that historically called itself "European" and that was so called by its neighbors. European culture must look elsewhere than in itself for what defines it.

Call to the Absent

I will say therefore to Europeans: "You don't exist!" There are no Europeans. Europe is a culture. Now, culture is a work on oneself, a formation of oneself by oneself, an effort to assimilate what goes beyond the individual. In consequence, it can not be inherited. It must on the contrary be conquered by each. One can not be born European, but one can work to

Culture- a) not something into which one is merly born
b) the necessity of an effort of appropation.

become one. One knows the sarcastic phrase of Friedrich Schlegel:

> The Germans, one hears it said, are as to the development of their artistic sense and of their scientific spirit, the first people in the world. Admittedly – only there are very few Germans.[13]

One can apply an analogous test to the pretended "Europeans." European culture is what defines the Europeans. But how many of those who live in Europe or elsewhere are at the height of that culture?

Turning myself at present to the non-Europeans, I would say: "You don't exist either!" There are no non-Europeans. The entire world, for its happiness or unhappiness, has been overrun by Europeans, and will remain affected by the European (in the neutral sense), by phenomena come from Europe. And before these, the rest of the world – if one can so speak of them – is in the same situation as those who are "already" European, or believe themselves such. If one understands by "Europeans" the current inhabitants of a certain space on a map, they can differ in many ways from those who live outside that space. But there is one way to which, on the level of principles, the two groups are on the same level. And that is just their Europeanness. If Europeanness is a culture, all are at the same distance from what they have to acquire. Europe, in the geographical or economic, etc., sense of the term, does not have to present itself as a model. It must on the contrary propose to itself, as it proposes to the rest of the world, Europeanization as a task.

All are at the same distance, but, to spin out the metaphor, not all are necessarily in the same direction. In other words, the obstacles are not the same, and it is important to be conscious of the difference. The danger for the inhabitants of the

---

13 F. Schlegel, Kritische Fragmente, §116; KA, t. 2, p. 161. This witticism conceals a full-fledged "speculative sentence" à la Hegel: the predicate goes back to the subject and determines it.

space that is called "European" (the pretended "Europeans")
is to consider that their Europeanness is a possession and no
longer something to conquer, a guaranteed income and not an
adventure, a particularity and not a universal vocation. From
this point of view, the interest in the past is an activity that
needs to be examined carefully. Indeed, there exists a retroac-
tive imperialism, by which a country claims what happened
on its current territory as belonging to it. As if cultural goods
existed in a sort of strong box, separated from the process by
which one appropriates them. But where do these goods
exist? There, where one edits the texts or the scores, where
one studies them, plays them, reproduces or performs them.
There, in a word, where one considers them as alive and capable of teaching us something that we would not be able to get
from our own resources. And nowhere else. One cannot take
cultural goods except by giving to them of oneself – except in
giving oneself to them.

The danger for the inhabitants of other spaces (the pretended "non-Europeans") is to see only the most superficial
characteristics of the mode of life, present or past, of the
inhabitants of the "European" space. If they want to
"Europeanize" themselves, the danger is of aping the *way of
life*, what is thought appropriate, in the interior of a certain
space. One lacks here what made it possible, the nourishing
soil in which it grew – not, perhaps, without exhausting it,
and even destroying it. One lacks what constitutes the mainspring of its dynamism, the potential difference of altitude in
relation to an external and superior source. Thus for example,
can one desire to borrow modern science and technology and
at the same time reject the turn of spirit that gave birth to
them?

Suppose, on the contrary, that the "non-Europeans"
attempted another way than that of Europeanization; the
danger would be that of caricaturing the model they wanted
to keep at a distance. It is even easier to do it in that neither
the past nor the present of what pretends to be Europe has

anything entirely rosy. One will have no trouble condemning the imperialism of Europe, its "materialism," and even the "desiccating" character of human relationships, etc. – all faults that many of Europe's inhabitants recognize, themselves deplore, and which they try to remedy. One forgets in this that the model from which one draws inspiration is beyond Europe, above it, that is the measure by which it is judged. One misses in this, in any event, the dynamism of European history, the movement that drove Europe upward, toward universalization.

The "non-Europeans" have in any event a non-negligible advantage over the Europeans, that of being conscious of the distance which separates them from Europe (real or imagined), of that painfully felt distance whose courageous admission has been the mainspring of European dynamism. As a result, it could be that Rome is no longer in Rome, and that the "non-Europeans" are fundamentally better able to take on the Roman attitude that has been Europe's good fortune, and to become more European than those who believe themselves already to be European.

VIII
The Roman Church

We have seen how Europe is "Roman" in its relationship to its two sources – the Jewish and the Greek. The "Roman" relation to the Jewish source defined Christendom in relation to Islam (ch. III). The "Roman" relationship to the Greek source defined Latin Europe vis-à-vis Islam, but also in relation to the Byzantine world (ch. IV). It gave to European culture a paradoxical relationship to what is proper to it (ch. V), and de-centered it in relation to its identity (ch. VI), imposing on it as a result a determined attitude toward what is its own (ch. VII). In this last chapter, I will place myself in the very interior of the European experience. I will examine here the role which that religion played which has marked Europe in a most decisive manner, that is to say, Christianity. I will show once again that Christianity is essentially "Roman." Finally, since there is a Church that one calls "Roman," that is the Catholic Church, I will say some words about the last of the dichotomies whose presence I noted, that is, that which opposes the Catholic Church to the world that issued from the Reformation.

"Roman" Catholicism?

The thread once again will be Romanity. A Church exists that, although this term has no place among the four "notes" that

it classically claims in its Credo ("one, holy, catholic, apostolic"), received the denomination "Roman." The Catholics
understand by this that the unity of the Church resides in the
communion of the successors of the Apostles around the successors of Peter, bishop of Rome. Now, is the fact that the
Pope has his seat in Rome purely contingent? Yes, if one
understands by that the intersection of a latitude and a longi-
tude. But the answer must be more nuanced if one takes into
account the symbolism the name of that city carries. On the
existence of an objective tie, adversaries and defenders of the
Catholic Church are agreed, even if they place the accent elsewhere, relaying the affects that I have evoked above.[1] For the
former, the Papacy is the heir of the will to power of Roman
imperialism;[2] the latter will say, for example, in taking over an
old argument of St. Augustine, that the unity of the inhabited
lands, established by Roman legions, was a preparation for
the evangelism of the Church.[3]

The question that I will pose here is to know to what
extent the Catholic Church merits the adjective "Roman." But
I will take this adjective in the sense that I have tried to elaborate. Since, for me, this adjective defines the European experience, my question will come to a sort of examination of conscience: I ask whether the Catholics can be, to reuse an expression of Nietzsche, ironically reused by Husserl, "good
Europeans."[4]

If one wonders now how to characterize Catholicism, one
must begin with a warning that will oblige us to make a correction in our vocabulary: "Catholicism" does not exist. In
any event, not in the sense that it would be an "–ism" as one
speaks of Marxism, of liberalism, or of *fulanismo* ("any-such-

1   Cf. ch. II, p. 28 f

2   One can think here of Dostoievski and of the story about the grand
     inquisitor in the *Brothers Karamazov*.

3   One still finds the idea in Dante, *Banquet*, IV, 5, 4.

4   Nietzsche, starting with *Human, All too Human* I (1878), 8, §475;
     Kritische Studienausgabe, vol. 2, p. 309; Husserl, *op. cit.*, p. 348.

ism") dear to Unamuno. Catholicism is not a system of thought, a school, yet less an ideology. "Catholic" is first of all a characteristic of the Church, one of its "notes." It is not a man, me for example, that is Catholic; it is the Church to which he belongs – and which his sin forbids him from identifying with perfectly. I will take "Catholicism" here, therefore, in a precise sense: I will understand by this what causes the Church to be catholic, or, if one may be permitted to say it, the catholicity of the Church.

The Problem of Culture

It does not seem to me to be too audacious to consider Catholicism as a species of the genre "Christianity." It will then be necessary to wonder if Catholicism is "Roman," either a) uniquely in itself – for example, because it would have remained faithful to the Pope in Rome at the moment when the Reformed Churches were drawing away – , or whether b) because its genre, Christianity, is already Roman itself, or whether c) at the same time because it is a species of Christianity, and because it adds to this genre a determination that is proper to it. My thesis will be that Catholicism consists in nothing more than in accepting the Christian faith up to its final consequences. If it is "Roman," this will then be to the extent that it pushes the Romanity intrinsic to Christianity all the way to the end. And not, for example (to summarize in simplifying an idea one finds in, among others, Maurras), in that it corrects a Christian movement that was originally revolutionary through the Roman sense of the social order. Therefore, we will have to examine in what way Christianity is "Roman." Such an inquiry has already been sketched above (ch. III). It seems to me, however, opportune to reconsider the question afresh.

I must therefore risk a provisional characterization of Christianity. It is not a question of pretending to describe it in all its dimensions, even in a summary fashion. I propose here to grasp it in function of the problem at hand, which is that of

culture. Christianity seems to me to represent a certain synthesis, a certain way of conceiving the relationship between
two terms. These two terms are, roughly, the divine and the
human. Or, if one prefers, God and man, the sacred and the
profane, heaven and earth, the spiritual and the temporal.
Each culture is concerned with these terms. Each culture proposes, explicitly or implicitly, a response to the question of
their relationship. Each culture proposes to articulate one
with the other in a certain way. In this domain, Christianity is
no exception. The question it confronts is the same that all
cultures confront.

But this question is resolved by it in a paradoxical fashion.
I will state it briefly: *Christianity unites the divine and the human
just where it is easy to distinguish them; it distinguishes the divine
and the human where it is easy to unite them*. It reunites what is
difficult to think of together, and it separates what is difficult
to think of as separate.

The divine and the human are easy to distinguish where
it is a matter of assigning to them an ontological statute. To
speak in the language of myth, God is in his heaven, man on
his earth. It is still by means of these images that the Psalmist
expresses himself: "Heaven is the heaven of YHWH; the earth
he gave to the sons of Adam" (Psalm 115:16). If one wants to
speak like the philosophers, one would say: God is outside of
time – he is eternal; man, on the other hand, is subject to the
passing of time – he is born, ages, and dies. Or again: God is
all-powerful, man is weak. Nothing, then, is easier than to
oppose, term by term, the attributes of God and the characteristics of man. A God so defined as the absolutely Other will
necessarily have to be indifferent to the world of men. This
would be the unmoved Prime Mover of Aristotle, too perfect
even to perceive the world, less noble than it.[5] Or again, these
would be the gods of Epicurus, who live in the region

---

5   Aristotle, *Metaphysics* Lambda, 9. Cf. my "Aristotle's God: What is He
     Doing?" in D. Conway and P. Kerzsberg, eds., *The Sovereignty of*

between worlds, where nothing comes to trouble their insou-
ciance.[6]

Reciprocally, the divine and the human are easy to unite
where it is a matter of assigning a domain of action to them.
The fundamental dimensions of human existence, such as
sexuality, political existence, etc., possess a sacred dimension
for man: Eros draws all living beings out beyond themselves,
in the direction of the future, their progeny, for whom they
are ready to sacrifice themselves.[7] The city can also excite,
when its own existence is in question, the enthusiasm of its
inhabitants, who may be ready to sacrifice their lives for it. It
is some time now since Fustel de Coulanges underlined the
religious dimension of the ancient city,[8] and more recent
researches, even if they have raised questions about his conclusions, still base themselves on territory he conquered. In
all cultures, the sexual and political realities possess a sacred
dimension. They possess it in themselves, and have no need
to receive it from elsewhere. The spiritual is not distinguished
from the temporal – to such a point that it is never even perceived as an independent reality. The king is at the same time
the priest of the city; the father of the family is at the same
time the priest of his home-altar.

We therefore have two symmetrical temptations: a certain
way of separating the divine and the human, a certain way of
uniting the divine and the human. This temptation is very
natural. Indeed, it only, if one may say, "cuts along the dotted
line" that underlines the divisions which present themselves
in reality. Or, inversely, it only draws together the mortises
and tenons which correspond to and invite one another. One
will separate the divine and the human where they are

Construction. Studies in the Thought of David R. Lachterman (Amsterdam:
Rodopi [Value Inquiry Book Series], forthcoming).

6   Epicurus, Letter to Herodotus §76 ff.

7   Plato, Symposium, 207a–b.

8   N. D. Fustel de Coulanges, La cité antique (1864).

already separated by their level of being. Inversely, one will unite them where they cooperate already.

Paradoxical Distinction and Union

Now, Christianity refuses these two temptations. And it answers them, as has been said, by an inverse effort in both directions. Let us begin with the distinction: Christianity distinguishes what would be easy to unite. It distinguishes the temporal and the spiritual, the religious and the political. One can oppose here Christianity and the Islamic world. The first refuses to be, like the second, a "religion and political regime" *(dîn wa-dawla)*. Good Muslim observers, like Al-Biruni, Averroes, or Ibn Khaldûn, have noted this refusal, which for them was a fault, and considered that it originated in the absence of the idea of the "holy war" *(ǧihād)* and of a politics that one could draw directly from Holy Scripture.[9] This refusal can be explained by historical facts: the Christian faith imposed itself despite, and even against, the Roman Empire, and did not conquer the State, but the civil society, and the State only through its intermediary, and at another time. However, this refusal also established itself on the level of principles.

This came first from its Jewish heritage.[10] Judaism freed itself from the primitive connection, still attested in the Old Testament (cf. Deuteronomy 2:12), that associated each people to its respective god in such a way that the attachment to the god constituted a people as a political entity. The ambiguous attitude in relation to monarchy, visible in the stories of

9 The strongest text on this is without doubt Ibn Khaldûn, *Muqaddima*, III, 31 (Q, vol. 1, p. 415, 3–18; R, vol. 1, p. 473). Cf. my essay "Trois regards musulmans sur la cité chrétienne," *Le Trimestre psychanalytique* 1996, pp. 9–21.

10 Cf. my article, "Judaïsme (période classique et médiévale)" in *Dictionnaire de philosophie politique*, ed. P. Raynaud and S. Rials (Paris: Presses Universitaires de France, 1996), col. 303–6.

Samuel's choice of Saul (1 Samuel 8, etc.) set in place a lasting antagonism between politics and religion. The exile put an end to the Kingdoms. The Temple was destroyed, and with it the connection between the faith of Israel and a material place, situated on the territory of a determinate State. In this way, the political pole of the antagonism disappeared. As a consequence, the religious membership of the people of Israel ceased to coincide with the political membership in a State. And the civil law of the states could be recognized in this way as legitimate in its proper domain; according to the adage, "The law of the kingdom has the force of law" (*dina de malkuta dina*).[11]

In Christianity, from the beginning, this distinction was founded in the preaching of Jesus. It was formulated in the words of Christ on the necessity of rendering to Caesar what belongs to Caesar, and to God what belongs to God (Matthew 22:17 and parallels). It took root, more profoundly, in the whole attitude of Jesus toward a messianism of a political or military nature: the refusal to allow himself to be made a king (John 6:15), and the will to accept as crown only a crown of thorns. The purely religious nature of what Christianity claimed to bring had as a consequence a refusal to charge the details of the rules governing inter-human relationships with the weight of the Absolute.

One sees it in the episode in which Jesus refuses to make himself the arbiter in a question of heritage:

> Someone in the crowd said to him: "Master, tell my brother to share [our] heritage with me." But he said: "My friend [man], who established me over you as judge and in charge of the sharing out?" And he said to them: "Look well and beware of all cupidity, because even for the one living amidst abundance, his life does not depend on what he disposes of." [Luke 12:13–15]

Jesus refused to be like Moses in every point by applying to himself the question posed to the latter (cf. Exodus 2:14).

11   On this adage, cf. *Jewish Encyclopaedia*, vol. 6, col. 51–55 (S. Shilo).

The text has no clear parallel in the Rabbinic literature.[12] And one does not know very well whether it is a question of an authentic *logion* or of an attribution from the primitive community. The content is not clear: was it a matter of recommending that one remain in joint possession, etc.?[13] However, retrospectively, and from the point of view of the history of culture, the passage is very interesting, and all the more so as it was a matter of an inheritance to share. One knows that it remains one of the most delicate domains of Muslim religious law, a rich source of cases for the students of *fiqh*. Everything happened as if one had here, before the letter, the radical exclusion of any Christian *shariah*. In consequence, the interhuman rules will not be charged with the weight of the Absolute, but left to the cares of men. The Absolute will bear only on the moral exigencies that ought to be the norm of all the juridical rules.

Christianity has never ceased appealing to this attitude based on principles. It has had to do it against all the temptations to absorb the political into the religious or the religious into the political. These temptations have sometimes come from outside, when the political power has sought to take over the religious power. But they can come from within just as easily, as when clerics want to use a spiritual influence for temporal ends. One has noticed it in diverse styles: earlier in Caesaropapism, and quite recently in certain currents of "liberation theology." These temptations have been more or less successfully avoided, and there is no question of declaring all the members of the Church innocent of any incursion outside of spiritual bounds. But when one demands, for example, as with the modern movement for the separation of Church and of State (of which secularism is only one version), that the

---

12 See Strack-Billerbeck, *Kommentar zum Neuen Testament aus Talmud und Midrash*, vol. 2, p. 190.

13 Cf. D. Daube, "Inheritance in Two Lucan Pericopes" in *Zeitschrift der Savigny-Stiftung für Rechtsgeschichte*, Romanistische Abteilung 72 (1955), pp. 326–29.

Church not leave its proper domain, one does not thereby apply a rule that would be foreign to it. All to the contrary, one brings it back to fidelity to a principle that arises out of its proper tradition.

The separation of temporal and spiritual, present on the level of principles and of historical origins, had been confirmed, and the Evangel, taken at its word, by the historical circumstances of the propagation of Christianity in the Roman Empire: its diffusion took place against the political power. The transition of the Imperial authorities to Christianity was the political consequence of a diffusion that was not brought about by political means. Despite the political translation of the supremacy of Christianity after first Constantine, then Theodosius, the idea that the religious domain and the political domain are distinct would never leave Christianity in general.

Popes and Emperors

As to the Catholic version of Christianity, I said in the beginning (ch. I) that Catholicism understood itself as the other of the Byzantine Orient. One can support here this characterization of Catholicism on a historical given. It furnished the concrete illustration of the second characteristic of Christianity, that is, the refusal of an unwarranted synthesis of the divine and the human in the human sphere. This illustration appears through the permanence, in the history of Europe, of the conflict between the Pope and the Emperor that materialized in the Middle Ages. While in the Orient the Byzantine Emperor, who besides received liturgical prerogatives at his coronation, made and unmade the Patriarchs, the Occident followed another course. This may have been for reasons that one can consider as purely historical contingencies, and even as completely bad (the Pope was also a head of state, had privileges to defend, etc.). The fact remains that, in the Latin Occident, a non-conflictual union of the temporal and the spiritual, which was not less dreamed of here than elsewhere ("union of the throne and of the altar," or the theocratic dreams of certain Popes, etc.), has never been a historical reality. In Byzantium, the situation was less clear. Admittedly, the temporal and spiritual were not at all confused. And each of these two principles had a social and institutional basis: opposite the basileus were the monks. But monasticism was not opposed to the emperor on the same level, as a power to another power. Within the Byzantine framework, the idea of a "symphony" (a harmonious agreement) of the temporal power of the Emperor and of the spiritual power of the Patriarch tended to confound the two much more than in the Occidental theory of the "two swords." In actuality, the Russian Orthodox clergy was brutally forced into submission to the Tsar starting with Peter the Great. In contrast, the Pope has always constituted, in the Occident, an obstacle to the ambitions of emperors and kings.

This conflict is perhaps what has allowed Europe to maintain that singularity which has made it a unique historical phenomenon. Its importance was clearly seen by Lord Acton, who wrote:

> To that conflict of four hundred years we owe the rise of civil liberty. If the Church had continued to buttress the thrones of the king whom it anointed, or if the struggle had terminated speedily in an undivided victory, all Europe would have sunk down under a Byzantine or Muscovite despotism.[14]

It was this conflict that prevented Europe from changing into one of those empires that reflected an ideology in their manner and in their image – whether they produced it or pretended to incarnate it. Indeed, on the one hand, it was the independence of religion in relation to the political that per-

---

14 "The History of Freedom in Christianity" (1877), *Selected Writings of Lord Acton*, ed. R. Fears, vol. 1 (Indianapolis, Ind.: Liberty*Classics*, 1985), p. 33.

mitted Europe to open up like a ripe fruit and to transmit its religious content to other cultural domains, even once political ties were broken. And on the other hand, the profane domain and its order received, in turn, a space at the interior of which they could develop according to their proper laws.

This does not mean that the profane order could unfold without any reference to ethics. One must understand rightly here what "render to Caesar . . ." means. The expression did not at all signify that the authority of God would be limited, and even excluded from a domain that men reserved to themselves. "What is Caesar's" is in a sense nothing, since Caesar himself possesses power from higher up, as Christ reminded Pilate (John 19:11). To say that what is Caesar's must be returned to him is not therefore to untie him from any obligation to justify himself before a jurisdiction that transcends him, to allow him to unfold according to a purely Machiavellian logic. It is completely to the contrary. Caesar is recognized the right to do what he can do and knows how to do. But the spiritual power, without marshalling the smallest armored division, reserves to itself a right over the temporal power. It is up to the spiritual power to remind the temporal of the absolute character of the ethical demand, one that judges the ends and the means of the temporal power. Ethics constitutes the framework of the profane order. But as any framework, it only limits negatively, without imposing positive directives.

Union and Distinction as Consequences of Secondarity

We have seen how Christianity distinguishes what one might be tempted to confound. Let us now see how it unites what one might be tempted to distinguish. In face of the temptation, contrary to the former one, of assigning to the divine and to the human distinct and incommunicable spheres, Christianity professes the incarnation. It is the only religion to do this, it seems, since the Indian idea of a divinity that undergoes avatars doesn't have a great deal to do with the Christian idea of incarnation. Let's allow it all its scope: a man, who lived in a precise time and place on the globe, that is, Jesus of Nazareth, is God. The habitual oppositions between the divine and the human are then no longer valid. God is capable of "descending" from heaven to earth, of entering in time and leading a temporal life here; he can know suffering and death. The Christians even go so far as to say that God reveals himself nowhere else more divine than in this abasement. From this point on, man is no longer hovered over by God. He is rather subverted by Him: God is no longer "over" but "under" him. We will have to return to the consequences of this fundamental doctrine.

Thus, Christianity's effort is first of all oriented toward a distinction to practice. It aims equally, as we have said, at a union. I have not tied these two aspects in an arbitrary fashion, for the sole pleasure of symmetry. Therefore, it is important to recall here that, if this effort is deployed in two directions, it results from one and the same source. A system is formed from the way the distinction of domains and the union of domains work.

I would now like to show how both distinction and union are the consequences of something at the center of European culture whose presence I have tried to disengage, that is, of secondarity. As the term "Romanity" functions to indicate this attitude, it will be a matter of showing here once again the Romanity of Christianity. I therefore affirm: first, *the idea of incarnation forms a whole with religious secondarity;* second, *the idea of a separation of the temporal and the spiritual forms a whole with cultural secondarity.*

The idea of incarnation, in Christianity, presupposes that Christ is not any ordinary "divine man," a particular case of a law stipulating that every being must pass by stages of terrestrial life. The divinity, whose human version he is, is not included in this law of incarnation. He is the Son of the God of Israel, i.e. of a God who is absolutely other than man. Nor is he, as with the Gnostics, a God foreign to the world and who arrived from outside. On the contrary, the Son of God came into the world as to his "home" (John 1:11). Nor is he a stranger in relation to history: he did not arrive without preparations, but as the result of the covenant between God and men, recorded in the Law and recalled by the prophets. He is incomprehensible without the history of Israel. He who is incarnated is singularized as being the Messiah of Israel and the Son of its God. To profess the Incarnation, therefore, has two consequences for Christianity: first, the faith in the incarnation is the point where Judaism and Christianity are most radically opposed; second, it supposes, in its very affirmation, that he who is incarnated is just that same God of Israel. Secondarity and incarnation are therefore at once cause and consequence of one another.

One must note a paradox here: the secondarity of Christianity in relation to Israel does not make the incarnation into something subordinate, which one can call "secondary" in the banal sense of the word. It remains a unique and unsurpassable fact. First, because what is second in time is not always second with regard to the thing itself: in this case, the Word[15] that the Christians confess was made flesh is the one in which the world was created "at the beginning" (John 1:1). Second, and especially, it is this very secondarity of the fact of the incarnation in relation to Israel that assures its absolute character.

With regard to the separation of the temporal and spiritual spheres, it has already been remarked that it is explained by the duality of sources, Greek and Jewish, "Athens" and "Jerusalem," of Occidental civilization.[16] This remark is right, but it leaves the essential unexplained. For it does not explain

---

15   One should keep in mind here that "the Word" translates "le Verbe," which also means "verb." [*translator's note*]

16   Cf. for example, G. E. von Grunebaum, *Islam . . .*, *op. cit.*, p. 73 f.

why there are two sources, in other terms, why one has not eliminated or absorbed the other. Christianity has not experienced
the need to remake anew what was already well made in the
Pagan world, for example, the law or political institutions.
Nor what entered consequentially in its sphere of influence,
as for example the languages and cultures of the peoples who
converted. Christianity superimposed itself on what already
existed. It grafted itself on a civilization that was already
organized according to its own laws. In particular it did not
have to create a new political unity, for example in confeder-
ating elements that had hitherto been divided. From the outset, this furnished a model for the separation of domains. The
formed community, the Church, did not have to substitute
itself for what already existed. And, in the course of history, it
has had to assume civil tasks only in the case of a breakdown
of the temporal authorities.

Separation as Consequence of Union

In the second place, one must see how the union and separation we have spoken of are themselves tied by an internal
logic. I will suggest here the following thesis: *the emergence of
a profane domain, and its consequences in European history,
including the possibility of "secular" societies – and even of radical
atheism – is made possible by the idea of incarnation.* This thesis
does not pretend to be entirely new. The idea according to
which modern "rationalism" issued from Christianity is
found, for example, in Leopardi and, more than a half century afterwards, in Nietzsche. Both insisted on the habits, and
even the intellectual affects inherited from Christianity (a
scrupulous love of the truth, etc.) and that, according to them,
had been turned against it.[17] However, as to what concerns
me here, I am not looking for this influence on the level of the
mental or moral attitude induced by the Christian fact, but in

---

17 Cf. G. Leopardi, *Zibaldone di pensieri*, August 1821; for Nietzsche, cf. for
    example *The Gay Science*, §344.

this fact itself, such as it is expressed in the most central way in the idea of the incarnation.

This is a concentration of the divine in a singular figure, that of Christ. Everything that God has to say, all the Word, therefore, is given there. To borrow an expression of one of the Greek Fathers, changing the sense a little: "the Word condensed" (*ho logos pachynetai*).[18] Or, to follow Saint Bernard, the Christ is the "Abbreviated Word"(*Verbum abbreviatum*).[19] This fact has the consequence of breaking with the diffuse sacredness characterizing the ancient, if you will, "Pagan," world, but also the Old Covenant. If the Father gave everything in the Son, he has nothing more to give us and, as Saint John of the Cross dared to say, God remains as if silent.[20] The Incarnation therefore has as a direct consequence a certain "disenchantment of the world." The texts of the New Testament express this fact in saying that the "elements of the world" have lost their powers,[21] and more recent authors have expressed it poetically.[22]

One speaks freely of "secularization," and one understands by that the passage of certain realities from a sphere conceived of as sacred to the profane domain. But this idea

---

18   The expression is found for the first time in nearly the same sense in Gregory of Nazianzus, *On Epiphany* (*Patrologiae Cursus, series Graeca* 36, 313b). On its evolution, cf. H. U. von Balthasar, *Kosmische Liturgie. Das Weltbild Maximus' des Bekenners*, 2nd ed. (Einsiedeln: Johannes, 1961), pp. 518–20.

19   Cf. among others *Sermon for the eve of Nativity* I, 1; *Patrologiae Cursus, series Latina* 183, 87b and III, 8; *ibid.*, 98c: "*contraxit se majestas.*"

20   John of the Cross, *Subida del monte Carmelo*, I, 22, 5; *Biblioteca de autores cristianos*, Madrid, 1989, p. 201. I have commented on this text in "The Impotence of the Word: The God Who Has Said It All," *Diogenes*, no. 170 (June, 1995), pp. 43–67.

21   Cf. H. Schlier, *Principalities and Powers in the New Testament* (New York: Herder & Herder, 1961).

22   I am thinking here of the theme of the departure of the elves in Tolkien's *The Lord of the Rings*.

explains nothing. Indeed, there must still exist something like a profane domain, which does not happen of its own accord:

> In most decisive respects, such talk of "secularization" is a thougtless deception, because a world toward which and in which one is made wordly already belongs to "secularization" and "becoming-worldly." The *saeculum*, the "world" through which something is "secularized" in the celebrated "secularization," does not exist in itself or in such a way that it can be realized simply by stepping out of the Christian world.[23]

The birth of a profane domain that would make secularization possible is conceivable only on the plain left free by a divine withdrawal. And this withdrawal, for Christianity, is the reverse of a concentration in a singular figure.

One sees the paradox: the withdrawal of the sacred comes from its refusal to remain in its inaccessible transcendence, as is the case in the negative theologies sketched by the philosophers, for example in Neo-Platonism, or in non-Christian religions. On the contrary, it comes from its being fully given. This is what the Fathers expressed by the famous expression: "In showing Himself, He hides himself" (*phainomenos kruptetai*).[24]

If this is the case, one can wonder if the attitude of a militant "secularism," desirous of founding human history outside of any reference to God, is tenable in the long run. For my part, I would like to suggest the hypothesis that this "secularism" is engaged in a dialectic that leads in a tendentious fashion toward its own self-destruction. It is not certain that one

---

23 Heidegger, *Nietzsche*, vol. 2 (Pfullingen: Neske, 1961), p. 146. English tr. F. A. Capuzzi (San Francisco: Harper, 1991), vol. 4, p. 100.

24 Cf. Dionysius the Areopagite, *Letter 3*; *Patrologiae Cursus, series Graeca* 3, 1069b; commentary in Maximus the Confessor, *Ambigua*; *Patrologiae Cursus, series Graeca* 91, 1048d–1049a; application to the intellect in John Scotus Erigena, *De divisione naturae*, III; *Patrologiae Cursus, series Graeca* 122, 633c.

can pretend at the same time, first, to separate the public and private domains, confining the religious in the latter, and secondly, to deny the presence of the divine in a singular figure. In doing this, does not one risk favoring the resurgence of the diffuse presence of an impersonal "sacred"?

Whatever may be the case, in what concerns Christianity, one may examine here three aspects of this paradoxical union: the nature of the revealed object, the historical presence of God in the Church, and the carnal presence of God in the sacraments.

The Nature of the Revealed Object

What is revealed in Christianity is not a text. In particular, it is not a text that would be in principle untranslatable, because it is inimitable. This implies a distance in relation to other lines of thought. This is the case in relation to the Islamic religion, especially since the solution of the Mutazilite crisis by the affirmation of the uncreated character of the Koran.[25] We see this yet again in contrast to certain fundamentalist interpretations of the principle of *scriptura sola* in Protestantism. One must repeat it here, against a lazy habit that is too widespread: Christianity is not a "religion of the book." It is, admittedly, a religion that has a book, in this case, THE Book, that is, the Bible. It assembles the Old Testament and the New into an indissoluble unity. The latter constitutes a reinterpretation of the old-testamentary experience starting from the event of the Christ.

Despite all that, the revealed object is in no case the New Testament. It is not even a "message," which would be the words of Jesus. This object is his entire person: a human personality, the liberty that animates him, the action through which it unfolds itself and whose totality forms a life. This is

---

25 Cf. *The Encyclopaedia of Islam,* "*Al-Kur'ān,*" vol. V, 426ab (A. T. Welch).

concentrated in the Paschal event that is perpetuated through the sacraments of the Church.

The Bible is admittedly a word of God, but it is not THE Word of God. That is the incarnate Word and it alone. In Christianity, there is no "book of God." As a consequence, there is no sacred language. And, with greater reason, there is no sacred culture. What the incarnation makes sacred is nothing other than humanity itself. Christ presents himself as a singular mode, unique to live the human life. The sole "language" that he makes sacred is the humanity of every man, on whom the incarnation confers an unheard of dignity.

The consequence of this is an entire way of understanding culture, and first of all in its primary vehicle, the languages. These are not planed down and reduced to one supposedly normative language among many. They are open together to a Word that is none of them. The incarnation of the Word makes it translate itself into an infinity of cultures: the possibilities of new cultures and new translations remain open until the end of the world.

Historically speaking, the birth of Europe is tied directly to this possibility: when, after the great invasions, the newly arrived peoples requested baptism, there was no question of asking them to adopt a new language, except for the liturgy. And even there, the missionaries who came from Byzantium composed a liturgy in the vernacular for the Slavs. The languages of the "barbarians" were respected and judged worthy of welcoming the Evangel. This did not happen without resistance on the part of those attached to Latin, but the conflict ended with the official legitimization of the vulgar languages by decisions taken at the highest level.[26] It manifested itself in an effort to translate the Sacred Scriptures into the vernacular language, especially where it was very far from

26 Cf. P. Wolff, *Les origines linguistiques de l'Europe occidentale* (Paris: Hachette, 1970), ch. IV, "La tour de Babel," especially p. 118.

Latin. Thus we had, for Old High German, the harmony of the Evangels of Otfrid, after the Gothic translation of Wulfila, today lost. For Old English, there were the translations of Alfred the Great. Or finally, for Slavonic, those of Cyril and Methodius. The diversity of languages, and therefore of the cultures that make up Europe, comes from this. One can note here that this linguistic politics continued outside the frontiers of Europe when the missionaries who originated there set out to write grammars and dictionaries for the languages of the peoples they wished to evangelize.

Reciprocally, for Christians there has never been long, or seriously, a question of rejecting ancient literatures that nonetheless transmitted Pagan representations. Their masterpieces have been preserved, permitting, as we have seen, that uninterrupted series of "renaissances" which constitutes European history.

The Presence of God in History

For Christianity, God enters into history. He enters into it, which means that he is present without his deriving from it. There is a history of salvation, an economy of salvation – which is not self-evident since in the Islamic religion, for example, this notion is unknown.[27] History is heavy with the divine, but it is not the divine itself. History is not made sacred, dressed with a "meaning" that certain men could read, thereby legitimizing their power. But history is not indifferent to what happens within it. It is yet less, in Gnostic style, "a nightmare one tries to awaken from."[28] History is assumed in the divine without being confounded with it.

For Christianity, the source of all meaning is, in the last analysis, the Word, such as it "was at the beginning with God," and such as it "became flesh" (John 1:1–14). This Word

27   Cf. *supra*, ch. III, p. 59.

28   Stephen Dedalus, in Joyce, *Ulysses*, 1.

exists first as the reason and the meaning that precedes all the caprices of chance or human arbitrariness. But it exists just as decidedly as the ultimate result of a history of salvation that concentrates itself progressively on the election of Israel, and then on one of its sons. The Catholic Church is faithful to this rootedness in the Old Covenant. From that moment in the second century when it rejected the heresy of Marcion, it has refused any attempt to "cast off its moorings" in relation to it.[29]

The Paschal event, we said above, is perpetuated in the sacraments of the Church. In this way, the history of Christianity is not that of interpretations given to a foundation text. It is the history of the saints. In two senses: it is the history of the *sancta* (in the neuter), of the "saintly things," of the sacraments and of their effects; it is also the history of the *sancti* and of the *sanctae*, of the men and women who are the culmination of the Church's effort to assimilate itself to Christ.

This is why Christianity makes the history of God pass through the history of men: it is founded on the testimony of men, the twelve apostles, and only secondly on the texts of the New Testament that record the authorized testimony.

The Entry of God into Flesh

The idea of creation by a good God has as consequence the following thesis on the nature and the dignity of the sensible: sensible realities are, in themselves, good. They are worthy of admiration and respect. It is their very dignity, and not some pretended nastiness of their nature, that imposes the duty to use them well. European culture carries the stamp of what one might call, in exaggerating a little, the sanctity of the sensible. This can be seen in the history of the first centuries when Christianity had to define its position in relation to

29 Cf. *supra*, ch. III, p. 58.

other currents of thought at the end of antiquity. It placed itself, against Gnosticism and Manichaeanism, on the same side as the Rabbis of the Talmud,[30] and on the same side also as the dominant current of pagan philosophy, represented by Alexander of Lycopolis[31] and especially by Plotinus.[32]

However, Plotinus refused the incarnation and the salvation of the body: a resurrection with the body would be in vain, for the true "resurrection" must be, on the contrary, a deliverance in relation to the body.[33] The philosophers of late antiquity thus reproached the Christians for their "passion for the body."[34] In consequence, they especially founded themselves, to affirm the goodness of the world, on the beauty and order of the cosmos. Christianity, on the other hand, was founded on the coming of the Word of God in the flesh of Jesus. Thus, what it defends is less the goodness of nature as such than the goodness of what, in nature, is personalized in the human body. The as yet undivided Church applied this way of seeing in affirming, for example against Catharism, the fundamental goodness of the creature and of the bodily creature in particular.

For Christianity in general, the incarnation gave to humanity a dignity that was itself that of God. Indeed, it specified the idea of creation in the image of God, such as was affirmed in Genesis (1:26): the image of God in man is not one of his faculties. If this were the case, it would be the highest faculty, intelligence, for example. This would lead to making

---

30   Cf. G. Stroumsa, "The hidden closeness: the Church Fathers and the Sages of the Talmud" (in Hebrew), *Mehqarey Yerushalayim be-Makhsheveth Israel* 2 (1982), pp. 170–75.

31   Cf. Alexander of Lycopolis, *Contre la doctrine de Mani*, ed. A. Villey (Paris: Cerf, 1985), 364 pp.

32   Plotinus, *Enneads*, II, 9 [33]. Cf. Endre von Ivánka, *Plato christianus. La réception critique du platonisme chez les Pères de l'Eglise* (Paris: Presses Universitaires de France, 1990), pp. 115–23.

33   Plotinus, *Enneads*, III, 6 [26], 6, 71 ff.

34   Celsus in Origen, *Against Celsus*, V, 14; SC no. 147, p. 48; VII, 36, 42, 45 and VIII, 49; *ibid.*, no. 150, p. 96, 112, 122, 280.

humanity vary in direct proportion to one's intelligence, and would deny it to the stupid man.[35] For Christianity, the image of God in man is his humanity, in its fullness. What, in man, is assumed by the divinity goes all the way to the carnal dimension of the person: the Incarnation goes all the way to the end, down to the lowest, into the body. God took a body, and he addresses himself to the body. The human body enters in this way into an unheard-of destiny, since it is called to a resurrection. This destiny makes the body the object of great respect, a respect that becomes what God tied himself to in irrevocable fashion.

The Proper of Catholicism

In a sense, the Catholic Church does not consider itself able to have anything proper to it. To admit it would be to renounce the very fact of a claim to universality that is included even in its name. I am not locating myself here on the level of principles affirmed and formulated in dogma. And I am not distinguishing between what, in my opinion, ought not to be distinguished, on this level, that is, the Latin Catholic Church and the Greek Orthodox Churches – that, besides, themselves claim the "catholic" note.

As to what I have called the paradoxical distinction, that between spiritual and temporal powers, the Reformation provoked, in the Reformed world as in the Catholic, a drift toward the takeover of the national churches by the political authorities. This was especially the case where the Reformation was imposed by the arms to a refractory people, as in Sweden. But Luther had already devolved the tasks of ecclesiastical organization to the worldly authority of German princes. And Henry VIII had assumed them to the profit of the Anglican prince. It is interesting to note that, even

---

35 Cf. my essay, "Le déni d'humanité. Sur le jugement 'ces gens ne sont pas des hommes' dans quelques textes antiques et médiévaux," *Lignes*, no. 12, pp. 217–32.

in countries that remained Catholic, the possibility of under-going Reformation served sovereigns as means to blackmail the pope into transferring some of his power – and in partic-ular, his control over the Church's goods. One saw this in Austria with Josephinism. One has also seen it in the France of the "very Christian king," in the Gallican movement. Revolutionary France sought fundamentally the same subor-dination of the national Church to political power in its attempt at a "Civil Constitution of the Clergy." For its part, the Catholic Church has maintained the necessity of a separa-tion on the level of its affirmations in principle. Its concrete history coincides in large part with the history of papal efforts against the temporal power's temptation to confiscate the means which permitted it to apply pressure on the spiritual.

As to the paradoxical union, the Catholic Church pushed the idea according to which God entered into history to the extreme: the incarnation is irreversible. It is not an adventure (or an avatar) of the Word that finally withdrew from history, never again to figure in it except as an example. The Word left its indelible traces here. History contains within itself a place where these traces are perpetuated. It is the Church, the place of salvation, the temple of the Spirit, that has not ceased pre-serving the memory of Christ. This is seen in two points that are besides tightly linked:

a) As to the structure of the Church, the Catholic Church continues to organize itself around the bishops, the apostles' successors. It materializes around singular men, who bear a proper name, and who are singularized by the fact of their selection by other singular men. The Church has no existence outside of concrete individuals. This personal character pro-hibits it from defining itself in relation to an ideology, as a "party line."

b) As to the doctrine of the sacraments, the dogma of the Catholic Church confesses that the presence in the Eucharist of the body of the resurrected Christ is quite real. And in this sense that it does not depend on the subjectivity of the believ-er who affirms this presence at the moment he consumes the consecrated bread, but that it is given as an object of adoration, in a presence that perdures as long as the Eucharistic species are susceptible of being consumed.

All this constitutes the dogma of the religion that marked European culture in the most decisive fashion. What can one say, now, of its historically concrete expression, and of its impact on this culture? Has Catholicism played a particular role in the affirmation of the goodness of the sensible? The Catholic Church has no doctrine particular to it in this domain, and for it, the results that truly count are buried in the secrets of the heart. As to the cultural phenomena that are accessible to historical verification, they do not permit one to affirm an incontestable causal relationship. At the most, one can point out certain affinities, certain convergences. For example, there is a certain convergence between the Catholic countries and great painting. It may be that he who spoke of Velázquez's *Surrender of Breda* as a "military sacrament"[36] was more right than he thought. But this affinity is of the same order, unnecessary, and weakened by a thousand exceptions, as is the known affinity between the Reformed countries and music. In any event, convergences of this sort pose a problem of method: to what extent can a certain sensibility that one notices in Latin and Danubian countries, or in Ireland, come from their Catholicism? To what extent, on the contrary, did it preexist that Catholicism, communicating to it a certain tint that has nothing to do with the dogma, and is sometimes contrary to it? In this matter, it is difficult to escape from a certain circle, which is besides necessary. The relation to Catholicism is perhaps solid in architecture: the Baroque style, as art of the Counterreformation, permits an easy interpretation as an affirmation of the intrinsic goodness of a world that is nonetheless perishable and wounded.

If therefore one is determined to isolate what Catholicism has that is proper to it and to recapitulate it in its unity, one might perhaps look along the lines of a certain seriousness

---

36 Carl Justi, *Diego Velázquez und sein Jahrhundert*, I (1888), p. 366.

about the incarnation, of the flesh transfigured by the Word.[37]
The flesh is indissolubly the historical tissue in the apostolic
succession, a sacramental species, a living body, sensible reality. If one wants to look for literary illustrations for this attitude of respect for the flesh and the sensible, one can think of
Hopkins, of Claudel, and even, on the reflexive level, on
everything Péguy said about the "carnal."[38]

Christianity as Form of European Culture

One can draw some conclusions from these reflections that
invite one to rethink the place of Christianity in European culture. Everyone admits the evidence that it is largely present
here. And one has pointed it out for good and bad reasons, to
congratulate it as well as to complain about it. One may consider, then, that it is a part of the *content* of European culture;
it constitutes a part of it alongside other elements such as,
principally, the ancient or Jewish heritage.

Now, inversely, I have tried to show how Christianity,
more deeply, constitutes the very *form* of the European relationship to its cultural heritage. According to me, the
Christian model of the attitude toward the past, such as it is
founded on the religious level in the secondarity of
Christianity vis-à-vis the Old Covenant, structures the whole
of this relationship.

I would therefore like to underline what meaning the
effort to maintain, and even to accentuate the Christian presence in Europe can have in this context. If this presence affected solely the content of European culture, as one element

---

37 On the medieval concept of flesh, cf. my essay, "A Medieval Model of
    Subjectivity: Toward a Rediscovery of Fleshliness" in *The Ancients and
    the Moderns*, ed. R. Lilly (Bloomington: Indiana University Press, 1996),
    pp. 230–47.

38 Cf. for example, in *Œuvres en prose*, Bibliothèque de la Pléiade, vol. 2,
    "A nos amis . . . ," p. 42; "Clio . . . ," p. 249; "Note sur M. Bergson . . . ,"
    p. 1340 ff; "Note conjointe sur M. Descartes . . . ," p. 1418.

among others, one would have to wonder why it should be assured a greater weight than another. It would be necessary to choose, for example, to privilege Christianity in relation to Judaism or Paganism. The reasons for this that one might allege would be more or less convincing. For one might point out that, on the level of principles, any choice is mutilating, and as to the choice of history, that the development of Christianity occurred at the price of repression of other models of culture that have remained purely virtual. One can underline this point in a polemical framework, and recall that this repression has been sometimes violent.[39] But even the spirit best disposed to Christianity would not know how to escape from the nostalgia that appears everywhere it has been necessary to choose between several possibilities, and therefore to keep only one.

In reality, if the thesis of this essay happens to be true, one must pose the problem in an entirely different fashion. For me, Christianity is, in relation to European culture, less its content than its form. In consequence, far from having to choose between diverse components of it, where Christianity appears as one among many, it is the presence of Christianity that has permitted the others to survive. In certain cases, one can put one's finger on the phenomenon. Thus, one can recognize to its glory as well as to criticize it (which is done by the Protestant side), that the Catholic Church has historically functioned as a conservator of Paganism in European culture. It was the art of the Renaissance, itself made possible by Patristic and medieval allegory, that has assured the "survival of the ancient gods" (J. Seznec). But Paganism is neutralized in it, more exactly preserved in its "demonical" moral neutrality. An attempt to resurrect Paganism outside of Catholicism quickly takes on suspect characteristics, and even entirely demoniac ones. One can verify this in a nearly tangible way by comparing the authentic Greek statues or

---

39 Cf. Nietzsche, *Der Antichrist*, §59; *Kritische Studienausgabe*, vol. 6, pp. 247–49.

their Renaissance imitations with the copies of the Foro Italico (the ex-Forum Mussolini) in Rome, or with those of Arno Breker.

If this is the case, an effort in favor of Christianity has nothing of the partisan or the self-interested. For with it, the whole of European culture finds itself defended.

IX
Conclusion:
Is Europe Still Roman?

The preceding essay proposed, with the liberty that this literary genre permits, to carry out a reading of the cultural history of Europe. It was not a matter, however, of taking yet another inventory of its content, but of reflecting on the meaning of an adventure or of an experience. My aim is not to invite the European to cast a satisfied eye on accomplished results. I would rather like to propose to him, with the concept of "Romanity" that I have tried to disengage, a model of cultural practice that seems to me to have lost none of its immediacy, or even of its urgency.

In concluding, I would like to consider here to what extent the model I am proposing can still be valid as a norm. And first, what could prevent us from following up on the adventure. Therefore, I would ask what are the threats that weigh on Europe. Not the diverse problems that may beset the Community of Fifteen or more: these external problems, such as the economic competition of the Far East, the collapse of a part of the Leninist world, the misery of the Third World, or internal problems, such as weak birthrates, the assimilation of immigrants, the degradation of the educational system, etc., are (perhaps) threats for Europe as a geopolitical reality.

Now, in this essay, I have concerned myself only with Europe understood as a cultural reality. I know that this does not float in an ether of pure ideas, and that it requires a sane, concrete basis, in particular where the culture impinges on the political domain – in education. But I prefer to leave the care of this foundation to those more competent, in order to consider myself only what could prevent Europe from remaining or from becoming itself once again: what threatens, if one may say it, the Europeanness of Europe – according to me, what threatens its "Romanity." I will give here only a sketch, to which one day I will perhaps return.

Marcionism and Modernity

One will have noticed that the historical references of the present essay were borrowed especially from Antiquity and the Middle Ages. This was, first of all, of course because this is the domain I know least imperfectly. But there is also a deeper reason: Europe constituted itself in the Middle Ages by distinguishing itself from its different "others." I have no intention at all of encouraging the dream of a mythical Middle Ages during which Europe and Christianity would have been united in an organic society without conflict. This was a legend fomented by the nostalgic romanticism of a pre-revolutionary society.[1] The historians have for a long time now treated this notion as it deserved.

But, even if it has been exorcised, the question remains inevitable: if Europe constituted itself in the Middle Ages, and supposing that modernity is a farewell to the Middle Ages, is modernity a danger for Europe? One must ask an entire series of questions here: is modernity a rupture with the Middle Ages? Is modernity on the contrary in continuity with it, and therefore its legitimate heir? And even, what is modernity? It

---

1   Novalis, *Christendom or Europe* (1799). For the context, cf. the sketch of P. Kluckhohn, *Das Ideengut der deutschen Romantik*, 5th ed. (Tübingen: Niemeyer, 1966), p. 126 ff.

will be understood that I cannot pretend to resolve these questions, or even to ask them correctly, in the framework of this essay.[2]

One can touch on the problem from the perspective of a concept I used above, that of Marcionism.[3] Are we witnessing a return of gnosticism, and in particular of Marcionism? I note the existence of a debate that I cannot enter into here.[4] Eric Voegelin has attempted to consider, not only certain tendencies of modernity, but the whole project of modernity, as a resurgence of gnosticism. Besides, he hardly named the particular Gnostics against whom the Fathers struggled, and in particular, said nothing about Marcion.[5] Hans Blumenberg, on the contrary, has characterized the Middle Ages as an effort to go beyond gnosis, but an effort that has stopped short. Its failure explained in large part the necessity of the passage to modernity, hence, according to the title of a fundamental work, the "legitimacy of modern times."[6]

One can distinguish two Marcionic characteristics of modernity: in relation to history and in relation to nature.

---

2   Cf., while waiting for something better, my essay "Le problème de l'homme moderne" in *Charles Taylor et l'interprétation de l'identité moderne*, ed. G. Laforest and P. de Lara, Entretiens de Cerisy, June 1995 (Paris: Cerf and Québec: Presses de l'Université de Laval, 1998), pp. 217–29.

3   Cf. *supra*, ch. III, p. 57 ff.

4   Cf. J. Taubes, "Das stahlerne Gehäuse und der Exodus daraus oder ein Streit um Marcion einst und heute" (1984) in *Vom Kult zur Kultur. Bausteine zu einer Kritik der historischen Vernunft* (Munich: Fink, 1996), pp. 173–81.

5   E. Voegelin, *The New Science of Politics. An Introduction.* (Chicago: University of Chicago Press, 1952), 193 pp., especially ch. IV, "Gnosticism – The Nature of Modernity" and p. 126, ". . . the essence of modernity [is] the growth of gnosticism."

6   H. Blumenberg, "Theologischer Absolutismus und humane Selbstbehauptung," second part of *Die Legitimität der Neuzeit* in *Säkularisierung und Selbstbehauptung* (Frankfurt: Suhrkamp. 1974), p. 143 ff. See my article "La galaxie Blumenberg" in *Le Débat* 83 (1995), pp. 173–86.

Historical Marcionism

I have characterized above the attitude of total rupture with the past, considered as having nothing at all to teach us, as being cultural Marcionism.[7] Now one can wonder if modernity would not be particularly threatened by this heresy. This is, in any event, what must happen if modernity is inseparable from an idea of a progress that would permit the granting of a permanent leave to a supposedly obscure past. This idea of progress forms a system with the historicization of the past that has already been briefly evoked.[8] Indeed, one must not let the completed past slide into oblivion, but rather immobilize it in memory so that progress can test its proper reality by measuring the distance traveled.

If the Romanity of Europe has preserved its relation to Hellenism, it seems that this relation is on the point of being lost. We often imagine that we have nothing to learn from a classical source, and in consequence, nothing to teach to barbarism. Admittedly, studies of the ancients can continue to nourish a significantly numerous body of philologists and historians. But, first, the classical reference is not self-evident for even the cultivated public; second, at the interior of the specialized cadres of the students of "classics," the very idea that certain texts can have a "classical" value has receded in the name of the real or pretended objectivity of a purely historical viewpoint. Nearly no one dares to maintain that the Ancients have something to teach us. The sources of European culture are put on the same level as those of other civilizations. This abandonment can be explained by the same phenomenon of compensation that we have seen above[9]: the end of the privileges granted classical studies is contemporaneous with decolonization. To hear it implicitly drummed

---

7   Cf. *supra*, p. 111.

8   Cf. *supra*, ch. V, p. 102.

9   Cf. *supra*, ch. II, p. 41 f.

into us that we are barbarians in need of civilization, without being able to catch up to the natives, would be insupportable.

Now everything takes place as if a certain equilibrium between the feeling of superiority and the feeling of inferiority reestablished itself at just another level, but without constituting, in what follows, a tension capable of engendering a dynamism. There is nothing left, short of a mixture of non-superiority and non-inferiority. A certain feeling of guilt before a leadership which nothing justifies any longer rubs shoulders with a more or less avowed disdain of the supposedly "under-developed." The dream of philology was to make us become Greek once again. This dream came to pass, but in an ironic fashion. We wanted to jump over the Romans so that we ourselves might become models of culture. But in doing this, we have suppressed the distance between Greek and "barbarian" that constituted Romanity itself, a distance which permitted the acculturation. We have thus become barbarians, no longer Hellenized barbarians, but barbarized Greeks, only half conscious of their own barbarism. The European expansion has brought in its wake, throughout the past, the diffusion of a culture with a universal vocation. This has managed to detach itself from the European conquerors, and even turned itself against them. But if imperialism today consists in nothing more than imposing one's own mode of life on others, the particular mode of life of a geographical region and a determinate economy, it no longer has any legitimacy.

Technical Marcionism

Modern technology rests on the postulate that the world must be remade. This supposes that it is badly made. In this way, modernity has accepted a fundamental premise of gnosis: the natural world is bad, or in any event, is not good. The science of Galileo and Newton made it impossible to see the physical universe as being governed by principles analogous to those governing our actions.[10] We are an exception – and perhaps only an apparent one – in a universe governed by pure relations of force. The modern science of nature obliges us to admit the moral neutrality of its object. But it heals the wound that it opens to the extent that it permits at the same time the correction, by technology, of what is imperfect in nature.

It is interesting to note that this vision of the world coexists with Marcionism in certain of its most important representatives. Thus, Spinoza, who reabsorbed into the laws of nature in general the exception that man seemed to constitute, is also the author of the *Theological-Political Treatise*, which implied a rejection of the Old Testament to the advantage of what he calls the Christ. Schopenhauer, who established the conviction that the universe is bad in European thought at the end of the nineteenth century, defended the gnostics and approved the Marcionist enterprise of a separation of the two Testaments to the sole advantage of the New – interpreted as drawing toward Buddhism.[11]

Are We still Romans?

Relation to History

The loss of an explicitly sought-after contact with the ancient sources seems real to me. It even seems to me to be regrettable. A world in which direct access to Homer or Virgil would be the province of specialists only seems to me singularly impoverished, and I have associated myself in efforts that have been deployed in favor of classical studies.

But this loss does not seem to me to be the most serious. This relation to the ancient sources is fundamentally only the

---

10   For the context, cf. my essay *La sagesse du monde. Histoire de l'expérience humaine de l'univers* (Paris: Fayard, 1999), 333 p.

11   Cf. *Die Welt als Wille und Vorstellung* II, addition to IV, 48, p. 791, 796 ff.

paradigm of something more general, that is to say, of cultural secondarity, the "Roman" attitude. Graver still would be the loss of that potential difference between a classicism and a barbarity that seems to me to constitute the driving force of Europe. Classicism (the "Hellenic" pole) can occur elsewhere than in the maintenance of Greek heritage; barbarism, similarly, can be interior[12] and its conquest has no need to organize itself in imperialism and colonialism. The more serious question seems to me, therefore, to be one of knowing if the founding gradient still exists.

The danger for Europe cannot come from outside for the simple reason that it cannot conceive of itself as an "inside." The danger lies in just this way of seeing: once one considers oneself as a closed space separated from others, what is on the exterior can no longer appear except as a threat. One sees an echo of this in the problems tied to immigration: the importation of laborers gives rise to a phantasm of an invasion of an "interior" by an "exterior" of supposedly questionable purity. However much Europe may conceive of itself in this way, it shows that it no longer believes that what it has to offer is likely to interest those who chanced to be born outside its frontiers.

Thus, the danger for Europe would be to stop returning to the model in relation to which it knows itself to be foreign and inferior, in order to preach its own virtues, to give itself out as an example in its particularity. What would be serious would be if Europe considered the universal it carries (the "Greek" of which we are "Romans") as a local particularity valid only for Europe, one which has no extension to other cultures. Now, one sometimes hears said, for example, that liberty, the rule of law, the right to bodily integrity, would not be good for certain peoples whose tradition, supposed to merit an infinite respect, is for despotism, for official lying, or mutilation – as if liberty and truth were local idiosyncrasies, to be considered

---

12 Cf. M. Henry, *La barbarie* (Paris: Grasset, 1987).

on the same level as the wearing of a kilt or the eating of snails.

It may be that the temptation cannot be exorcised unless the Christian Church continues to oppose it with just as firm a refusal on the most fundamental level, by remaining conscious, in its relation to the Old Covenant, of its secondarity. Indeed, we have seen that secondarity in the religious domain is not a question of time: the Old Covenant is not a past from which one distances oneself, but a permanent foundation.[13] Therefore, it does not enter into the dialectic of progress and of historicization, a dialectic from which, in contrast, the relation to the "classical" past cannot escape. It is on this level, then, that one must preserve the most vivid consciousness of it.

Relation to Nature and to the Body

We can no longer be pagans in the sense that nature has lost for us the evidence of its goodness. The conviction of the goodness of the universe and of its good order lasted with hardly any contest from Antiquity to the end of the Middle Ages. One can no longer still affirm this in the age of technology. Despite the inadequate way in which he understood the Greek gods, Marx was right at least on this point: we can no longer believe in the Olympians now that we can produce the effects that were once attributed to them.[14]

But well before technology prevented us from believing in the pagan gods, Israel received the injunction not to participate in their cult. The prophets delivered themselves over to a demythologizing of the natural powers in refusing to bend their knees before them, whether it was a matter of celestial bodies or of the elements of vegetal and animal fecundity (springs, atmospheric phenomena, sexual organs, etc.). They

---

13 Cf. *supra*, ch. VI, p. 110 f.

14 Marx, *A Contribution to the Critique of Political Economy*, tr. S. W. Ryazanskaya (New York: International Publishers. 1970), p. 216 f.

were reduced to the state of what had been created in function of man. One sees it from the creation story that opens our Bibles: the sun and the moon are no longer even named, but reduced to the status of lights and measures of time. Christianity did not retreat from this radical demythologization.

It brought in a determinate attitude before nature. A nature that is no longer considered as sacred becomes accessible to every man, whose function then becomes to dominate nature. This was not a question of submitting nature to man's caprices in exhausting it, but of using it as an instrument of the acts of freedom that man alone is able to assert. One must therefore claim a Christian legitimacy to the technological use of nature.[15] It may even be that the demythologization that Christianity has carried with it has played a role, not only in the development of technology, but also in the development of the modern science that has made technology possible. By constraining Europe to leave the universe of pagan antiquity, Christianity in effect contributed to making a new physics necessary, one that would rest on concepts other than those of a Greek physics of Aristotelian inspiration. This is perhaps what one can discover in the polemics of John Philoponus against it.[16]

But one should then reaffirm the body's goodness. First, as a biological reality – supposing that the perspective of biology suffices to exhaust it, and even to grasp the body as a phenomenon. And especially, as personal reality. And Christianity has something to offer here. It could be that the Catholic Church possesses in addition, in its affirmation of the body's goodness, a precious secret, and of a burning urgency, needed in a period when the human body, once con-

---

15 Cf. J.-M. Garrigues, *Dieu sans idée du mal. La liberté de l'homme au coeur de Dieu*, 2nd ed. (Paris: Desclée, 1990), p. 27 ff.

16 One will recognize here the central thesis of P. Duhem presented in his monumental work, *Le système du monde*, and continued in the work of S. Jaki.

sidered as pure machine, faces the threat of unprecedented aggression as a consequence of progress in genetics – not from the outside, but from the inside, by an attack aimed no longer at destroying it, but one that pretends to reconstruct it according to a determined plan.

Within its tradition, Christianity possesses an adage on grace that does not suppress nature, but which makes it more perfect (*gratia non tollit, sed perficit naturam*). One could apply this principle to the technological relation to nature. It is not a matter of adoring a nature become divine, nor of dreaming of withdrawing from a nature made devilish, but of instituting a supple relationship to it. Technology can admittedly perfect nature, but there should be no question of its suppressing that in which nature reaches its height: the human body as the place of the incarnation and as a support of the individual.

Perhaps one has to appeal here to something one might call a third Romanity. It would no longer be located in relation to a "Jewish" religious heritage or to a "Greek" cultural heritage, but in relation to nature. It would be a question, here also, of recognizing ourselves as the heirs and debtors of a wisdom and a revelation which preceded us: the "wisdom of the body" (Nietzsche), and the appearance in the flesh of a personal face.

Christianity and the Future of Europe

Christianity, including its Catholic version, has been able to play a role in the early stages of the European Community through the faith of some of its protagonists. One has often noted it: Konrad Adenauer, Robert Schuman, Alcide de Gasperi were, as Christians, convinced of both the profound unity of their civilization and of the radical malice of international relations founded on violence. But the Christian faith did not intervene in the construction of Europe in the sense that it could furnish recipes that would permit the resolution of one or another technical problem in a satisfying fashion.

Not that this dimension is base or subordinate. On the contrary, it is essential, and it even seems to me that the refusal of an ethereal spiritualism is rather a mark of the Catholic spirit. It is very desirable that Christians attempt to resolve the concrete problems of modern society. But in the analysis of these problems, their faith shines no special light for them.

On the other hand, it may be that Christianity can help give something imperceptible to the construction of Europe. And this is nothing less than the very object of that construction. For how can we be quite sure that what is being constructed is truly Europe, and not simply a free trade area, or a center of power, defined only by its geographical position and by the name that it accidentally received, a "little cape on the Asian continent" (Valéry)? For Europe to remain itself, it is not necessary that everyone who inhabits it recognize explicitly that they are Christians, yet less be "militants." The "dream of Compostela," that of a reconquest (and by what means?), seems to me to exist only in the heads of those who denounce it. One must nonetheless wonder whether Europe can dispense with those elements that we have tried to set out above without denaturing itself.

Europe must remain, or become once again, the place of the separation of the temporal and the spiritual, and moreover, of peace between them – each recognizing the legitimacy of the other in its proper domain. It must remain, or become once again, the place where one recognizes an intimate relationship of man with God, a covenant that descends to the most carnal dimensions of humanity, that must be the object of an unfailing respect. It must remain, or become once again, the place where the unity between men cannot occur around an ideology, but in the relations between concrete individuals and groups. If these elements were completely erased, one might have constructed something, perhaps even something lasting – but would this be Europe?

I do not know if Europe has a future. I believe, on the other hand, I know how it could prevent itself from having one: a Europe that would set itself to believing that what it carries is worthwhile only for itself, a Europe that seeks its identity in withdrawing into what is particular to it (for example, into a cheap "Indo-Europeanness") would cease to merit to have a future. The cultural task that awaits Europe today could therefore consist, according to the sense that I have discussed, in becoming Roman once again. If Europe has to become aware of itself once again, it will have to show both – if I can mobilize two languages this time in a truly European pun – *Selbstbewußtsein* and *self-consciousness*. These two seeming synonyms in fact designate contraries. We may translate them in applying them to Europe: it must at once be conscious of its value and of its unworthiness – of its value in the face of an internal and external barbarism that it must control; and of its unworthiness in relation to that of which it is only the messenger and servant.

Postface

The idea of writing this essay was given to me, of course, by the prospect of European unification. It has already provoked a reflection that is not limited to showing that everyone will find it profitable. It has equally invited one to consider the past of Europe and to reread it from the point of view of its near unity. Several recent good works (for example, the work of K. Pomian) have attempted a history of Europe or of the European idea. I can only refer to them for what amounts to the historical sub-basement that I presuppose.

My aim is different, and the treaty of 1992 (Maastricht) was only the pretext. Indeed, I am trying to consider here what the essence of Europe is, what it is fundamentally. But to do this, I have not proposed to list an inventory of the content of European culture, to perform a "spectral analysis" in the fashion of Keyserling. I am not seeking to measure the contribution of each religious or national tradition, and yet less that of individuals. Those that I happen to cite appear only where they can shed some light on my sole object.

This is not the *content* of European culture, which I have treated only in oblique fashion, but only the *form* of that culture. For me, it is a question, in regard to the transmission of that content, of drawing out into the open the internal dynamism that makes the European cultural adventure possible. It is this mainspring that I have qualified as "Roman." As will be apparent, it is less a question of Republican or Imperial Rome than of an aspect of the cultural history, or even of the myth of Rome, that I have isolated and generalized.

I have pointed out, on the one hand, its past fecundity. But I also wish to help keep it from running dry. It is not therefore a matter only of describing a past, but also of projecting a future in (re)proposing for Europe a model relationship to what is proper to it.

I do not picture myself speaking from nowhere, and the reader has the right to know who addresses him, what my point of view is, where to locate what I know more or less badly. I am therefore French, Catholic, a philosopher by formation, a professor by trade. My domain of research, starting from Greek thought, is currently oriented toward the Middle Ages, especially the Jewish and Muslim Middle Ages.

My origins explain certain accents and certain silences, and most especially my very intention in writing this essay. As a European, writing on Europe, I am a party engaged in what I am speaking about. Despite my concern for objectivity, which I impose on myself as the ethical concomitant of every writer, I cannot dream of being entirely unengaged by these ties.

My nationality and my formation explain the place occupied by French references, or a certain preponderance of Germanic and Anglo-Saxon cultural domains over the Latin and Slavic ones. My trade explains the place given to the transmission of philosophical heritage over other dimensions of culture (ch. IV). My religious affiliation explains my insistence on the role of Christianity in the formation of Europe (ch. VIII), and my attempt to highlight the contribution of the Catholic Church (p. 172 ff.).

My origins also explain a certain modesty: I have hesitated to speak at length on the Orthodox and Protestant worlds, whether to evaluate their positive contribution to European history or to measure their responsibility for the more somber dimensions of that history. I have preferred to leave to the care of each to vindicate their past or to sing their own dirges. On the other hand, my subject has obliged me to speak of Judaism and Islam, seen from the perspective of their cultural influence. I have done it with the maximum of respect, but inevitably, from the outside.

I do not, however, want to reduce what I have said to the expression of some vague "sensibility." I claim to provide arguments that should be judged on their merits.

*

One may be surprised to find in a work that presents itself as an essay an apparatus that sets it off from the looser rules proper to this literary genre: abundant annotations and full of bibliographical references, along with an index. I am not in any way trying to display my erudition: experts will have no trouble seeing that, on many points, it is second-hand. On the contrary, I would like to place at the disposition of the reader, each time I have noted a little known fact, something to verify me by, and indicate the scholar from whom he could learn more.

On the other hand, I have not cited everything I have read, and yet less everything that I ought to have read. Similarly, I have taken the liberty of citing books in the editions that I have at hand – sometimes in the original, sometimes in translation.

Several of the ideas that I develop here have been sketched for the first time in texts that appeared elsewhere, in particular:

"L'avenir romain de l'Europe," *Communio*, IX-2 (March-April 1984), p. 123–30. Italian trans. in *Identità culturale dell'Europa. Le vie della pace* (Turin: Aic, 1984), pp. 147–53.

"Christianisme et culture. Quelques remarques de circon-stance," *Communio*, XI-2 (March-April 1986), pp. 46–63.

"L'Europe et le défi chrétien," *Communio*, XV-3 (May-August 1990), pp. 6–17. Castillian trans. in *Catolicismo y cultura* (Madrid: EDICE, 1990), pp. 73–86.

"Les intermédiaires invisibles: entre les Grecs et nous, Romains et Arabes" in *Les Grecs, les Romains et nous. L'Antiquité est-elle moderne?* ed. R.-P. Droit (Paris: Le Monde Edition, 1991), pp. 18–35.

"Le fondamenti dell'Europa. Il cristianesimo come forma della cultura europea," trans. E. Tartagni in *Cristianesimo e cultura in Europa. Memoria, coscienza, progetto*, Atti del Simposio presinodale (Vatican, October 28–31, 1991) (CSEO, 1991), pp. 25–36.

Inversely, I have had occasion, after the two first editions, to be called to present my thesis orally or in writing. The following have been published:

"Christ, Culture, and the New Europe," *First Things* 25 (August-Sept. 1992), pp. 36–40.

"Les trente capitales culturelles de l'Europe," *Le Nouvel Observateur*, Dossiers, no. 13 (November 1992), p. 12.

"Europe, tous les chemins passent par Rome," *Esprit*, no. 189 (February 1993), pp. 32–40; German trans. G. Reisecker: "Europa: alle Wege führen über Rom," *Netz Europa*, H. Gsöllpointner (Linz, 1994), pp. 9–15; Hungarian trans., J. Török: "Európa: minden út Rómaba vezet," *Communio*, Nemzetközi katolikus folyóirat, 1993, pp. 42–52.

L'Arche, Mensuel du judaïsme français, no. 428 (April 1993), p. 88.

"A Europa das racionalidades," *Communio*, Revista Internacional Catolica (Lisbonne), XI (1994), pp. 358–64 (original French version unpublished).

"Grandeur et humilité des cultures," *Face à la création la responsabilité de l'homme. Rencontre entre l'Est et l'Ouest* (Novgorod-Saint-Pétersbourg: Mame/ACCE, 1996), pp. 150–54.

"L'incendie et l'aqueduc," *Le Banquet,* Revue du CERAP, no. 8, 1ˢᵗ semester 1996, pp. 38–49.

"Orient und Okzident. Modelle 'römischer' Christenheit," trans. A. Marenzeller in *Das Europa der Religionen. Ein Kontinent zwischen Säkularisierung und Fundamentalismus,*" ed. O. Kallscheuer (Frankfort: Fischer, 1996), pp. 45–65 and 325–27 (original English version unpublished).

"Die Geschichte der europäischen Kultur als Selbsteuropäisierung," trans. W. Seitter, *Tumult. Schriften zur Verkehrswissenschaft* (Vienna), "Europas Grenzen," 22 (1996), pp. 94–100.

"Sohnland Europa," P. Koslowski/R. Brague, *Vaterland Europa? Europäische und nationale Identität im Konflikt* (Passagen forum) (Vienna: Passagen Verlag, 1997), pp. 19–42.

"Inklusion und Verdauung. Zwei Modelle Kultureller Aneignung," G. Figal, J. Grondin, D. J. Schmidt, *Hermeneutische Wege. H.-G. Gadamer zum Hundertsten* (Tübingen: Mohr, 2000), pp. 293–306.

"Is European Culture 'a Tale of Two Cities'?" S. Stern-Gillet, M. T. Lunati, *Historical, Cultural, Socio-Political and Economic Perspectives on Europe* (Lewiston, N.Y.: The Edwin Mellen Press, 2000), pp. 33–50.

If I have neither wanted nor been able to do the work of a historian, it has nonetheless been necessary to take an overview of large blocks of history. Some competent friends accepted the task of rereading the manuscript, and kept me from certain blunders, repaired some omissions, and pushed me to clarify points that I had treated in too allusive a fashion.

This is the case with Marie-Hélène Congourdeau (CNRS, Byzantine History) and F. Guy Bedouelle, O.P. (Fribourg, Church History). My colleague Françoise Micheau (Paris-I, Middle Eastern Medieval History) has generously given her time to effect a careful grooming of the whole, and passed on many precious documents to me. In the notes, I have indicated by their initials what I owe directly. Philippe Cormier

(Nantes, Philosophy) and Guy Stroumsa (Jerusalem, Comparative Religion) have read the manuscript at different stages of its elaboration. Thierry Bert read my text as theoretician and practitioner of European affairs. Corinne Marion, whom I have the privilege to have as an editor, has done her work with conscience and kindness.

Everyone has pointed out to me precious corrections and details. I offer them my very heartfelt thanks. But I absolve them for any faults that may remain in this essay, as well as any complicity in its central thesis.

The title of the French edition, *Europe, la voie romaine*, is excellent. I feel therefore a bit sheepish to admit I did not find it myself, but happy to have the occasion once again to thank Jean-Luc Marion.

To my wife, finally, for having corrected the author and put up with the work – if it was not perhaps more the contrary – I dedicate the work which is only to give her her due.

A second version, enlarged and (I hope) improved, was published in February 1993. This latter version was the basis of translations into Catalan, German, Czech, Hungarian, Spanish, Russian, and Turkish. The present version has been enlarged once again and, I hope, improved yet more. I have integrated into it the remarks offered by a number of diverse readers, as well as my own second thoughts, sometimes published in the articles listed above. My Italian translator, A. Soldati, permitted me to correct several errors of reference. The present version has been provided to Greek, Slovenian, Rumanian, Lithuanian and Polish translators.

Boston, May 2001

Index

flesh 176
FONTAINE, R. 99
FONTIALIS, J. 85
form / content 31, 54, 103, 107, 176 f.
Franciscan movement 121
FREDERICK II OF SICILY 81
French 90, 138
FREUD, S. 50
FUCHS, F. 50
FUSTEL DE COULANGES, N. D. 156

GALEN 71
GALILEO 21, 183
GAMA, VASCO DE 85
GARDET, L. 117
GARRIGUES, J.-M. 187
GASPERI DE, A. 188
Gauls 28, 142
GELBLUM, T. 78
genealogy 132
GENNADIUS 19
GERBERT OF AURILLAC 81
Germany 12, 138 f.
AL-GHAZÂLÎ 61, 121
GIBBON, E. 36, 69
GIBBONS, W. R. 136
GILSON, E. 81, 94
Gnostic 57, 164, 170, 172, 181, 183 f.
GOETHE, J.-W. 26, 101
GOLDZIHER, I. 15, 60
GORKY, M. 57
GRABAR, A. 132
GRAETZ, H. 30
Greek 98 f.

SAINT GREGORY THE GREAT 83, 144
GREGORY OF NAZIANZUS 166
GREGORY OF NYSSA 84
GRIMAL, P. 37
GRÜNEBAUM VON, G. 9, 80, 96, 112, 118, 164
GUIDI, I. 117
GUILLAUME IX OF TOULOUSE 88
GUTAS, D. 76, 87, 108
GUTENBERG, J. 67

HADAS-LEBEL, M. 53
HADOT, P. 72
HAECKER, T. 53
HALECKI, O. 6, 10
AL-HAKÎM 47
HAMANT, Y. 19
HAPSBURG 28
HARDER, R. 33
HARNACK VON, A. 57
HASKINS, C. H. 115
HAY, D. 11, 35
Hebrew 36, 51
HEGEL, G. W. F. 33, 139, 149
HEIDEGGER, M. 20, 30, 67, 116, 167
HEINE, H. 25
HEINZE, R. 34
HENRY VIII 173
HENRY THE NAVIGATOR 85
HENRY, M. 185
HENTSCH, T. 13
HERGE 136
HERMARCHUS 74
HERODOTUS 3, 40, 144 f.